Southern cultures

Fall 2003
Published by the
University of North Carolina Press
for the
Center for the Study of the American South
at the University of North Carolina at Chapel Hill

Books

The Man in Question

When historian Anne Firor Scott shared some vintage photographs with us for use with her essay "My Twentieth Century: Leaves from a Journal" [Spring 2003], we discovered among them many hidden treasures. We especially liked one striking snapshot that captured 1921 downtown Athens street life, which we made our cover photo. She was kind enough to write us a short letter telling more about the picture.

The children, grandchildren, and great-grandchildren of the man on the cover of the Spring 2003 issue are delighted by it. Perhaps a word of explanation is in order: the man in question is John William Firor Sr., who was, in the early 1920s, county agricultural agent for Clarke County, Georgia. Later he was invited to establish a department of agricultural economics and rural sociology at the University of Georgia, a post which he held until retirement. His lifelong concern with the needs of Georgia farmers is reflected in the photograph: he had initiated a farmers' market (called a "curb market"), which took place every Saturday on the main street of Athens, Georgia. The photograph was taken on the day the market opened, and as its father, so to speak, he had the privilege of buying the first ear of corn.

Anne Firor Scott

Chapel Hill, North Carolina

The man in question on our Spring 2003 cover is none other than historian Anne Firor Scott's father.

Ed. note: Email SouthernCultures@unc.edu or send your correspondence to "Letters to the Editors," Southern Cultures, CB#9127, UNC-CH, Chapel Hill, NC 27599-9127. We assume letters received at this address or by email are intended for publication, subject to editing. If we use your letter, we'll send you a free extra copy of the issue in which it appears.

front porch

Novelist Elizabeth Spencer writes hauntingly of two divergent experiences from her childhood in Carrollton, Mississippi. One chapter of her memoir, *Landscapes of the Heart*, tells of Miss Beauregard Somerville, an imposing dowager who lived in a big white house and ruled the leading families with an iron code of propriety. A word from Miss Beaurie could cover the shoulders and extinguish the cigarettes of the most daring young ladies, and even for the youngest child, scratching oneself in her parlor was too horrible to contemplate. Thinking of harrowing visits to that seat of judgment, Spencer remembers "the rustle of taffeta. Long skirts in hot weather or cold. Petticoats. Black shoes. High lace collars. And no one to doubt that she was right about everything." Even after Miss Beaurie's death, her

above:

In an interview never before published, former NEH Chair William R. Ferris talks with Eudora Welty about all manner of subjects, including her ties to Cleanth Brooks and even a private sailing excursion with William Faulkner. Cleanth Brooks and Eudora Welty at the dedication of a new Faulkner stamp, courtesy of the William R. Ferris Papers in the Southern Folklife Collection at The University of North Carolina at Chapel Hill.

judgments lived on, governing the lives and consciences of Carrollton's ladies with an iron code of convention. In this environment, Spencer recalls, life for young women was "as rigidly bounded as a high-security prison, guards on the watchtowers, dogs trained for hot pursuit. Manners and behavior, what one wore and did not wear, what talk was allowed and what was never to be mentioned (though everyone knew it). Gossip and confidences," she concludes, held an unbreakable sway.

Somewhat later in her memoir, Elizabeth Spencer describes her first day at school. Unlike the world of Miss Beaurie, she found school "strange to the last degree. I might as well have been in another state or even among Yankees, whom I had heard about but never seen. I could see our house from the edge of the campus, but it seemed to me I was observing it from the moon." The world of school was utterly different from the rest of Carrollton, and Spencer felt wistful about the changes it brought to her. But she leaves no doubt that the new world of learning brought a kind of emancipation she could find nowhere else. "From then on, life changed in a certain way I could not define," she explains. After she started school, "everybody, every single person, was just the same. Yet I was losing them; they were fading before my eyes." Echoing the famous sentiment of Thomas Wolfe, she remembers that school set her on a path that took her away from the Mississippi of her childhood, never truly to return, no matter what Miss Beauregard might say. "You can go somewhere, anywhere you want," she declares, "but you can't ever quite come back. Having gone up a road and entered a building at an appointed hour, I could find no way to come back out of it and feel the same way about my grandfather, ginger cakes, or a new book satchel. This was the big surprise, and I had no power over it."

It's probably safe to say that for many southerners, the grip of Miss Beauregard's rules still have a great deal of power. There are dos and don'ts and whole encyclopedias of order and control that have to be obeyed. These rules gain power from their reputation for permanence and antiquity. As Spencer remembers about Miss Beauregard's manners, "She couldn't have invented them herself, so she must have got them from those before her who knew best." Manners can cover everything. Clothing, liquor, and cigarettes. Church and family. Weddings, funerals, and politics. Race, class, and sex. Especially sex. Even in Carrollton, one suspects, the rules have relaxed a bit since Miss Beaurie held sway, but they have not disappeared. And for many of us, even the most liberated, the existence of these rules is sometimes a blessed relief. They allow us to go on autopilot in a time of stress, and transfer the burden of decision-making from fallible individuals to the time-tested wisdom of the folk. Let's face it, the world would be pretty chaotic with no rules at all.

But the imprisoning nature of tradition is modernism's oldest cliché. Almost universally, the southerners who can step back and describe traditional rules, their powers, and their costs are those who have somehow escaped their harshest strictures and lived to tell about it. For them, change is a kind of torchlight that enables them to see and describe what they have left behind. For the rest of us, tradition is so firm it can be virtually invisible until it shifts, appearing and disappearing in the same transient motion.

Our articles in this issue give examples of how change exposes tradition and its secrets, including the secrets of how tradition was created in the first place. The closest parallel to the changes described by Elizabeth Spencer come in an interview with her friend and fellow Mississippi author, the late Eudora Welty. Speaking with folklorist Bill Ferris in 1996, Welty talked fondly of old friends, of parties and travel, of Russian authors, of jobs far away. She scarcely mentions the word "South" and Ferris hardly asks her about it. But listening carefully, it is clear that Eudora Welty is telling us that she learned to chronicle her South by escaping tradition, not southern embracing it. Her parents came from out of state. She went to college in Wisconsin. She worked in New York. She applied the gracious gift of sociability—so carefully taught in southern families—to making special friends: Robert Penn Warren, Cleanth Brooks, Katherine Anne Porter, finally William Faulkner. Many thanks to Bill Ferris for sharing this precious conversation with one of the most outstanding literary figures of the twentieth-century South.

Barbara Hahn's essay on tobacco farming takes us far away from Welty's Mississippi, but tells much more than she lets on about the way a traditional world is created, literally from the ground up. An historian of technology, Hahn is interested in the ways that humans interact with their machines to create new environments that often go on to reshape their inhabitants and the machines they make. It turns out that the tobacco industry is a perfect example of how this process works. When you start with the tobacco plant and the delightful effects it has on smokers, but then add flue curing, tenant farming, racial inequality, existing land use patterns, federal price supports, the auction system, and a nearly infinite combination of soils, fertilizers, pesticides, and other devices, you get more than a complex of crops and tools. You get an entire rural way of life, every bit as complicated and tradition-bound as the cotton plantation world that elevated ladies like Miss Beauregard in small-town Mississippi.

To insiders and outsiders alike, the tobacco economy as it existed from the 1930s to very recently sometimes seemed as "traditional" and permanent as the law of the Medes and the Persians. In fact, the tobacco economy as we know it was constructed as recently as the New Deal and has been changing ever since, as farmers, scientists, inventors, equipment companies, cigarette companies, and extension agents have continuously worked to revise, reform, and reconfigure it to better suit themselves. Now even bigger changes are afoot, bringing the transient and even artificial character of the Tobacco South closer into focus.

Barbara Hahn wades into this story with energy and charm, utterly out of place

in a tobacco field, she tells us, but instantly at home within the calculations and creative energies of a world that is changing to survive. Using the story of her road trip through tobacco country to tell a larger story, Hahn makes us realize that continuous change brought this old-fashioned world into existence, even as more change may be dismantling it.

Vanderbilt University's Larry J. Griffin and Ashley B. Thompson tackle the theme of changing tradition more directly, by reviewing poll data about southerners and the South. While it's commonplace to observe that southern distinctiveness is fading, Griffin and Thompson show that the number of people calling themselves "southerners" has receded much more slowly than the region's vanishing "peculiar institutions." What does this mean? Certainly the South is changing, as it always has. Does that mean it's disappearing? Probably too soon to tell.

"Railroad Bill," Burgin Mathews tells us, was an African American outlaw who once terrified rural Alabama and stirred a ferocious manhunt in 1896. When a relentless posse finally killed him, Railroad Bill inspired a classic legend whose multiple variations eventually became a standard in the emerging repertoire of "folk" music, from "old time" guitar pickers to Joan Baez. It would be hard to imagine a character at greater variance from Miss Beauregard Somerville's remorseless gentility, but Railroad Bill reminds us that "tradition" can be the product of modernity and violence as much as manners and decorum.

After all, Railroad Bill got his nickname by robbing the trains that had recently penetrated South Alabama, brought in to haul away turpentine and timber after the pine forests of the upper South had fallen to beetles and the axe. The railroads and lumber camps had brought in masses of unattached black men looking for work, and they in turn brought dread to the existing white population. Historian

Edward Ayers found that lynching rates in the New South ran highest in places like Railroad Bill's Gulf Coast, where the African American population had grown most rapidly. The posse who brought the outlaw down, moreover, were aroused by newly radical rhetoric about the "black beast Negro," intensified by late-nineteenth-century political crises that led to Populism, disfranchisement, and Jim Crow. And the whole story spread among the "folk," not by ancient word of mouth, but by telegraph, press accounts, and commercially recorded music. Regardless of its timeless qualities, Mathews explains, the story of Railroad Bill is really a tale of modernity. And given the obvious connections between racial repression and the strict social and gender conventions upheld by Miss Beauregard, it's not hard to imagine that Railroad Bill and the later writers of the Southern Renaissance were fellow rebels under the skin.

The noted poet and fiction-writer Robert Morgan favors us with "Vietnam War Memorial," a treatment of war and its aftermath as reflected in that famous black-mirrored monument in Washington, D.C. We close with Elaine Neil Orr's "Not Forgotten," a reminiscence about a very different South—the African South of the Yoruba people. The child of Southern Baptist missionaries, Orr grew up influenced by two Souths: the distinctive Nigerian region that surrounded her and the exotic, distant South Carolina of her parents' birth and rearing. Her two Souths have much in common, a fact whose painful origins Orr cannot forget.

Once again, Orr's change in perspective makes an old reality visible as it vanishes, like the vision of an animal that can only see something when it moves. That kind of vision seems hard-wired for nostalgia, but perhaps it's better than no sight at all. It's the type of vision we've got, so we might as well enjoy the view. And once again, this issue of *Southern Cultures*.

HARRY L. WATSON, *Coeditor*

Eudora Welty

"... standing under a shower of blessings"

by William R. Ferris

Eudora Welty discusses her writing life and friendships in this previously unpublished interview.
Eudora Welty, courtesy of the William R. Ferris Papers in the Southern Folklife Collection at
The University of North Carolina at Chapel Hill.

Ed. note: William R. Ferris interviewed Eudora Welty at her home in Jackson, Mississippi, on March 3, 1996.

BILL FERRIS: Eudora, I want to ask you if you could reminisce about [Robert Penn] "Red" Warren and the friendship that you shared with him, and also with Cleanth [Brooks].

EUDORA WELTY: Well, our friendship was certainly warm and long lasting. Of course, they were so good to me from the beginning. When I was totally unknown, they encouraged me and helped me in every way. I was so indebted to both of them. You know, you didn't meet people like them, at least in my world. It was a long time before I got to meet them, either one. But when I did go down to Baton Rouge and met them down there, we had a grand time. And I felt so picked out, you know, so favored. They had published me in the *Southern Review*—I guess they were the first people to publish my work anywhere. So I felt that I was very close to them, even though we didn't meet very often. Then Red came and did a lecture one time over at Belhaven College across the street [from Welty's house in Jackson]. I was telling him about Ross Barnett, and he laughed so hard I thought he was going to strangle. He just loved all those political tales from Mississippi. He said, "Every time I think about that night I still laugh till my ribs hurt." But he loved choice things like that.

BF: Do you remember your visits with the Warrens when they were in Connecticut?

EW: I remember going out after programs at the [National] Institute of Arts and Letters. The Warrens invited me to come home with them, and that was lots of fun. I always had such a good time with Red, in particular, because his sense of humor was laid right around here, you know, Mississippi and our politics and everything.

BF: You've written about friendship, Eudora, and how important it is for writers. Could you tell us some more about your friendships with Mr. Warren and Mr. Brooks?

EW: Well, I was living in Jackson, just beginning to write, and it didn't occur to me to think about the world of writing. It's really like a little network. I just felt it was solitary to write. Just do a book, and somebody reads it. But they helped me realize what a network it is, a mutual learning society. Readers and writers everywhere. Just made me see the whole world of writing in a different way, in an exciting way. I was so ignorant that I didn't know how lucky I was. But of course I became more appreciative as I learned more. And you can multiply that by many people they were good to and helped.

BF: Including me.

EW: They lived in that world and it was just natural to them, if they saw something they thought was good, they did something about it. There are not many people like that, are there?

BF: Very few, and you are among them.

On Robert Penn "Red" Warren and Cleanth Brooks: "You know, you didn't meet people like them, at least in my world." With designs on photographing Cleanth, courtesy of the William R. Ferris Papers in the Southern Folklife Collection at The University of North Carolina at Chapel Hill.

EW: No. But they made all the difference to my work and to me, and I'm sure that's repeated in many other cases.

BF: Eudora, you are so closely associated with Jackson as a city. Can you talk about Jackson and your feelings for this city?

EW: Oh, I've always liked being here. My family, my father and mother, were both from away, and when they came here when they married, it was kind of adventurous for them. They were making a new life. And my father—he was a businessman—had decided that Mississippi was a place with a future. He was interested in, you know, civilized life and so on. I was the firstborn of the first generation in Jackson. He was from Ohio and my mother from West Virginia. I always felt very lucky—and they did, too—that they had come here. Growing up in Jackson was lovely at that time. We had wonderful school principals and teachers that I still remember with great affection and awe. It was a pleasant town to grow up in. I'm sure I was ignorant of all kinds of things. I had no political knowledge. My father was a Republican in Jackson. I don't think anybody but the Pullman porter was a Republican—he was a black man. You know, there weren't any Republicans extant around here. My mother was a Democrat. And of course they argued politically at the breakfast table. I early got an idea that there were complications about our system down here.

BF: The other city I want to ask about, where you spent time, is New York City.

EW: Well, it was always my dream city, of course. I went to Columbia's school of business just so I could be a year in New York and go to the theater. This was during the Depression. In fact, Roosevelt was elected while I was up there, I think. My father and mother were both sensitive. They wanted their children to be well educated, and you couldn't always be so. They wanted me to go where things were more exacting and liberal and understanding and I don't know what all. But they just wanted me to have all of that, and I did too. I went to the University of Wisconsin, which then was run by Mr. Glenn Frank [president, 1925–37], isn't that his name?

BF: Yes.

EW: "This is a college, not a country club"—that was their motto. This was in the twenties. But wasn't I lucky? So I did get a good education, and I was very grateful to them and glad they knew it at the time. I'm glad it didn't just come over me later. I felt very aware of my blessings at that time. I think partly because I saw how miserable things were down here, and I could see the difference.

BF: Eudora, can you talk about other Mississippians and southerners who were in New York that you knew there?

EW: I didn't know any to begin with, because I was just a schoolgirl. Who did I meet?

BF: Lehman Engel was one.[1]

*"I always had such
a good time with Red,
in particular, because
his sense of humor was
laid right around here,
you know, Mississippi
and our politics and
everything." With
Robert Penn Warren
at the White House,
courtesy of the
William R. Ferris
Papers in the Southern
Folklife Collection
at The University of
North Carolina at
Chapel Hill.*

EW: Oh yes. He was an old Jackson friend, a wonderful person, and just open-armed with hospitality for anybody from Mississippi who went to New York. And he knew everybody in the arts, because he was in the musical theater. He was a conductor and a composer, and he knew people in the entertainment end. I remember once he told me, "Keep your eye out for a young man named Gene Kelly." I remember that. Lehman was a good friend from Jackson. He knew absolutely everybody in New York, I think, that would be of interest to a writer or musician. And he was so generous, shared everything, and gave everything.

BF:. I wanted to also ask you about Herschel Brickell.[2]

EW: He was from Yazoo City, wasn't he? A sweet, good man. I got to know him better down here than in New York. I did not go and look people up. I just couldn't do that. But Herschel was so kind and so abundantly helpful to peo-

"I was living in Jackson, just beginning to write, and it didn't occur to me to think about the world of writing."
Photograph courtesy of the William R. Ferris Papers in the Southern Folklife Collection at The University of
North Carolina at Chapel Hill.

ple. He knew Stark Young, who I knew was up there, although I never got to
meet him. I was much too shy. But I've been reading his correspondence. Have
you read that?

BF: Yes.

EW: Isn't it fine?

BF: Yes, beautiful.

EW: Just beautiful. I read his reviews, of course, in the paper. Such a learned man.
And I like to think of his living within a stone's throw of William Faulkner.
They could just call out to each other, I should think. I used to see him at the
theater. I had a job at the *New York Times* as a book reviewer. It was just a slight
job, but it kept me in the city. I could be there and get off any time I wished and
go to the theater. You know, it was just like a fairy godmother had given me
something I wanted. And that was when Stark Young was writing his southern
version of Chekhov. All kinds of things were going on up there, from our point
of view, and of course from every point of view. And Lehman's great friend
was the dancer Martha Graham. You could learn the whole world from her by

"I've always liked being here. My family, my father and mother, were both from away, and when they came here when they married, it was kind of adventurous for them. They were making a new life. . . . I was the firstborn of the first generation in Jackson." Photograph courtesy of the William R. Ferris Papers in the Southern Folklife Collection at The University of North Carolina at Chapel Hill.

going to her concerts. Mississippi had a regular little group. They all were tight-knit, self-conscious. They all knew each other and invited each other around. And they were good to us kids who were going to Columbia.

When you are young, I guess you don't realize how lucky you are. There I was, just put down in the middle of all these wonderful things. I just took it for granted. I thought that was being in New York.

BF: But you took full advantage of it.

EW: Well, I appreciated it. I would have been deaf, dumb, and blind not to see what was there. And besides which, I realized later how exceptionally generous they all were as people, you know, to the young.

BF: Eudora, did you know Katherine Anne Porter very well? Was she a friend?

EW: Well, when she was at the *Southern Review*, married to Albert Erskine, they invited me down to Baton Rouge. That was my first trip down there. I was petrified to go and meet her, but I did. She invited me to lunch, and that's how I got to meet her. She had always been kind to me in her work, and in promoting mine, and that was just like standing under a shower of blessings. This was the time Red was writing his political novel on Louisiana.

BF: *All the King's Men?*

EW: *All the King's Men.* And it was fun to hear them talking about it. Unbelievable, really.

BF: Yes.

EW: They were so generous and warm-hearted, those people were. I'm a shy person. I never would have approached them, but they wrote to me. That was part of their way. I'll never cease to be grateful.

BF: Eudora, were films important to you? Did you enjoy going to them?

EW: Oh, yes. I always loved films because you could go to them in Jackson when you were a child, movies of a certain kind. I always loved the film. Didn't you?

BF: I did, and do.

EW: It spoke to me, too. It spoke to me through the imagination. It was something you could do without any money to amount to anything. Now you have to pay untold money for a seat. But in those days, in Jackson, you could go for a quarter or something like that. I was lucky in every way, I think, growing up

"My father and mother were both sensitive. They wanted their children to be well educated, and you couldn't always be so. They wanted me to go where things were more exacting and liberal and understanding and I don't know what all. But they just wanted me to have all of that, and I did too." Photograph courtesy of the William R. Ferris Papers in the Southern Folklife Collection at The University of North Carolina at Chapel Hill.

in Jackson. Life here was so easy, and for a quarter you could go to the movies and see a cat man named Dr. Caligari.[3] Life was easy and simple. You walked where you went. I guess you look back on something through rose-colored glasses, but I know life was made easy for me and for my imagination. And also it just scared me to imagine whatever came next. Anyway, when I went to New York and Columbia, I did the same things. I went to the theater and the movies and read good books, of course. Like you, I had books in my family home that I could read, was encouraged to read.

BF: Eudora, when did you first feel that you wanted to write? When did you become aware of that desire?

EW: I don't remember a conscious decision. But I was a big reader, and I sort of thought in terms of the imagination and words. It was natural, I think, to want to write. But it's an entirely different matter to be a serious writer. I don't know when that began—I guess after I went to college at the University of Wisconsin. There were some good professors in writing and in literature who made me feel that I was in touch with something.

BF: Do you remember telling your parents that you wanted to be a writer? Was there a moment when you spoke with them?

EW: No. My father died young, and my mother always encouraged me to write. I

"I had a job at the New York Times as a book reviewer. It was just a slight job, but it kept me in the city. I could be there and get off any time I wished and go to the theater. You know, it was just like a fairy godmother had given me something I wanted." Photograph courtesy of the William R. Ferris Papers in the Southern Folklife Collection at The University of North Carolina at Chapel Hill.

"I was petrified to go and meet [Katherine Anne Porter], but I did. She invited me to lunch, and that's how I got to meet her. She had always been kind to me in her work, and in promoting mine, and that was just like standing under a shower of blessings." Photograph courtesy of the William R. Ferris Papers in the Southern Folklife Collection at The University of North Carolina at Chapel Hill.

think that she took it for granted that I wanted to be a writer, but I was pretty self-conscious about things. I knew she was behind me. And the fact that in those hard days of the Depression and all . . . she thought nothing of paying for me to go to Columbia. Without words, I mean, she was encouraging me and channeling me in the right direction.

I don't know what my father might have done. But he died so young. He was just fifty-two. He didn't live long enough to read anything I'd written in print, you know, anything professional. And I don't know whether he would have encouraged me or not. He was not much of one for fiction, as he told me. He thought that was not the real world, and that we should face up to what was out there. Maybe in the twenties that's the way people thought. He was smart, and he read all the time. I grew up in a house where they were always buying books and encyclopedias and dictionaries and things like that. And that was so lucky. I took it for granted, but that was the important thing.

BF: How did you first discover the camera and photography? Was that something you did as a child?

EW: Yes. My father was a photographer. He had nice cameras. I began to use a camera, too, and to develop film in the kitchen at night. The times were con-

ducive too. You know, the WPA [Works Progress Administration] came along and everything was in such poverty here. It was there to be photographed. Anybody could have seen it. Even I, as a child, could recognize it. It was telling its own story in human terms. I don't know what my father would have thought of my photographs because what he wanted was accuracy, and the actual picture taking—that was fine, that was part of it.

I know I am wasting your time because I'm just rattling on.

BF: No. This is beautiful. You spoke about imagination, Eudora, and how your family nurtured your imagination.

EW: They did.

BF: Can you talk about that?

EW: Yes, because from the beginning we had books in the family. My parents were both readers, with very different kinds of minds. My father was factual and historical, and mother was imaginative—fiction was what she liked to read. But we read in this house all the time, all of us did. I think that's the luckiest thing you can do for a child, don't you? I'm sure you had the same kind of family.

BF: I did. My father was like your father, very factual and practical, and Mother very emotional and imaginative.

EW: It was the same combination. And I can't imagine how different and bad life might have been to have grown up in a house where there were no books and no interest in the imagination or in the world around us, or what was happening in the world. We had that wonderful advantage.

"[My father] didn't live long enough to read anything I'd written in print, you know, anything professional. And I don't know whether he would have encouraged me or not. He was not much of one for fiction, as he told me. He thought that was not the real world, and that we should face up to what was out there." Photograph courtesy of the William R. Ferris Papers in the Southern Folklife Collection at The University of North Carolina at Chapel Hill.

BF: We've had an interesting exchange with our Russian friends, Eudora.

EW: Oh, wonderful.

BF: They have come here over the years. Do you see an affinity between the Russian writers and southern writers?

EW: Well, I don't know. I've enjoyed talking to the young Russian writers. I think that we have an affinity in that we both have a sense of the human problems in this world. I mean, the material out of which you would write interests both of us. But now it's so wonderful to be growing up and realize that you can have some insight into the whole world of people. I never knew that as a child, did you?

BF: No. What about the Russian writers like Tolstoy, Dostoevski, Chekhov, and others you read—did you find a kinship there?

EW: Well, I wouldn't have dared think that, but of course that's what led you on in reading them. You recognized so much, and you thought, "How good this

"But we read in this house all the time, all of us did. I think that's the luckiest thing you can do for a child, don't you?" Photograph courtesy of the William R. Ferris Papers in the Southern Folklife Collection at The University of North Carolina at Chapel Hill.

is," you know. "He understands." Well, this was just an ignorant person reading—I mean, a teenager, in the case of Chekhov, my favorite of all. And I learned so much from reading them—not only in the human way, but as a writer. It just opened up the whole world to read the Russians.

BF: Do you have any thoughts for a writer who is beginning a career as you did?

EW: Well, that word "career" will stop me. But as for the work you're doing for yourself, I think that's just right there for you to learn and find out, and that's what beckons you on and charms you. It's from reading, I'm sure. Learning what can be done in order to understand the world around you and how communication happens. But it all comes from inside, of course. Any writer writes from within, but reading is what opens up that world. I've never felt any different, and I'm pretty old now.

BF: No, you're not.

EW: In my eighties. I better hurry up and learn some more quick.

BF: I heard a story about Faulkner when a student asked him how to become a writer. Faulkner told him he should "go live in a garret and eat 'pa'ched cawn.'"

"You recognized so much, and you thought, 'How good this is,' you know. 'He understands.' Well, this was just an ignorant person reading—I mean, a teenager, in the case of Chekhov, my favorite of all. And I learned so much from reading them—not only in the human way, but as a writer. It just opened up the whole world to read the Russians." Photograph courtesy of the William R. Ferris Papers in the Southern Folklife Collection at The University of North Carolina at Chapel Hill.

EW: [laughing] Isn't that wonderful? He had the answer. That's just wonderful.

BF: You met Faulkner when you were in Oxford.

EW: I did. I never would have looked him up. But, you know, Miss Ella Somerville was a friend of his, and she invited him to dinner one night as a treat for me. I was up visiting in her house with some mutual friends from Jackson. He came, and also his wife, and—you knew Miss Ella, didn't you?

BF: No, I didn't.

EW: You must be too young. She was tremendous. She was one of the great ladies of the South, with a wonderful sense of humor, well-educated, and she had open house there for everybody—pictures on the wall that Stark Young had done for her—you know, she was just part of that world up there in north Mis-

"Any writer writes from within, but reading is what opens up that world. I've never felt any different, and I'm pretty old now. . . . In my eighties. I better hurry up and learn some more quick."
Photograph courtesy of the William R. Ferris Papers in the Southern Folklife Collection at The University of North Carolina at Chapel Hill.

sissippi. I didn't know she was going to invite Mr. Faulkner over. She did it as a surprise for me. He and his wife came to dinner, and I think there was one other couple. We just had a grand time. That was the way to meet him. I would have been petrified to just stand up and formally be introduced to Mr. William Faulkner.

It was very informal. We stood around the piano and sang hymns after supper (which we all knew, of course—the same ones). He didn't have much to say. But he did invite me to go sailing the next day. I was kind of scared to do it, but I did. How could I not have? They had just finished making that lake up there.

BF: Sardis Lake?

EW: Sardis, that was it. And he said, "Just be down there, and I'll come up in the boat"—he had made the boat, you know—"I'll come up in the boat, and you come out and get on it." And so I went out there, and you know there wasn't any shore? Do you remember how it was to begin with?

BF: The lake is still that way!

EW: It was nothing but a lot of "stobbs" around it, if that's a word, and these old trees. I didn't know what to do, and I didn't want Mr. Faulkner to think that I was so inept. So what I did was just walk on into the water and go on out and get in the boat. It was very simple. One, two, three. I just waded out in my—I don't know if I took my shoes off or left them on; it wouldn't have mattered— through the muck. And then I got in his sailboat. Of course I was wet, but you can't ask William Faulkner to wring you out, I guess. It hadn't occurred to me until this minute that I might have [laughter]. He didn't say anything. I didn't say anything. Neither one of us said a word. We took a long sailing trip, and it was real comfortable, you know. Nobody tried to make conversation. I'm sure he never made conversation. And I never got to know him well. But it was so kind of him to do that, and he was so much fun. I was so lucky I got to meet him. I never dreamed I would. Did you?

BF: No, I never did.

EW: You were too young.

BF: We drove by his home once when I was with my family, and we didn't stop. I thought about it, but I was too timid.

EW: I couldn't have done anything like that either. But people did. I used to get phone calls—I bet you do, too. "Do you have the ear of Mr. Faulkner?" "No sir." "How could I meet him?" "I have no idea."

BF: I get those same calls about you.

EW: Oh, no.

BF: They always want your phone number, and I say I don't have it, or I can't give it to you, but I will let her know that you want to see her.

EW: I am so sorry.

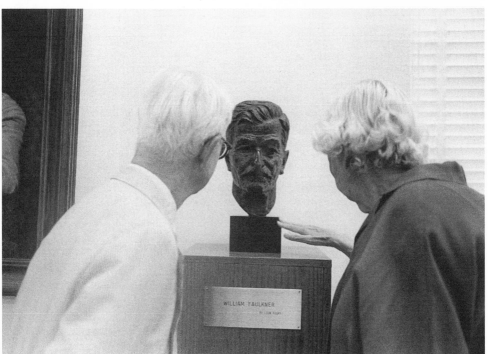

"I just waded out in my—I don't know if I took my shoes off or left them on. It wouldn't have mattered—through the muck. And then I got in his sailboat. Of course I was wet, but you can't ask William Faulkner to wring you out, I guess. It hadn't occurred to me until this minute that I might have." With Cleanth Brooks at the dedication of a new Faulkner stamp, courtesy of the William R. Ferris Papers in the Southern Folklife Collection at The University of North Carolina at Chapel Hill.

BF: No. I'm happy to take them.

EW: I'm not. I'm unhappy they call. I'm sorry.

BF: Do you remember Faulkner's home? Did you visit him at his home? What was that like?

EW: I've only been there a couple of times. It was very remote feeling, but maybe anything in that part of the county is. I don't know. I don't mean I was lonesome, but I felt it was very private. I felt sort of like an intruder, an intruder in the dust.

BF: You mentioned singing hymns with Mr. Faulkner. I remember when I came here once with Cleanth Brooks. When Mr. Brooks got out of the car, you came out to greet him, and you both held arms and sang a hymn as you walked together. I thought it was so beautiful.

EW: Oh, did we? What was it, I wonder?

BF: You were walking together in step, and I thought that's —

EW: That sounds so nice.

BF: — so lovely.

EW: I wonder what hymn it was. I don't know all that many. Do you?

BF: I don't either. I think maybe Mr. Brooks was leading.

EW: I expect he was.

BF: Eudora, thank you so much for sharing these memories. They are wonderful.

NOTES

1. Lehman Engel was a Broadway composer who was born in Jackson in 1910. He and Eudora Welty were lifelong friends, and their extensive correspondence is archived at Millsaps College and at the Mississippi Department of Archives and History in Jackson.

2. Herschel Brickell was a literary agent in New York whose correspondence with Eudora Welty is archived at the University of Mississippi.

3. *The Cabinet of Dr. Caligari*, a 1919 silent film by Robert Wiene.

Into the Belly of the Beast
The 2002 North Carolina Flue-Cured Tobacco Tour

by Barbara Hahn

 omeone in Chapel Hill actually thinks about tobacco?" I've heard this sentiment twice already today, but this time the speaker explains the surprise behind it: "Most days I think those folks don't know what supports them." I laugh my agreement, and we shake hands. She urges me to get a plate of dinner, pointing out that the hundred-odd people with nametags have already eaten. Besides, this is her home, and she insists. So I get a plate and fill it from the vats of meat and potatoes and green beans and corn. I grab a biscuit and a Styrofoam cup of iced tea, and take a seat. It's noontime on the second day of the 2002 North Carolina Flue-Cured Tobacco Tour. After our meal we're going down to the curing barns to see a state-of-the-art box-loading machine. The machine stands as the centerpiece of a prototype harvest-and-curing system that will get the leaf off the plant, precision-cured to its buyer's specifications, and out the door—all without the touch of human hands. At the moment, though, the system is still under construction: modified school buses serve to carry the tobacco leaves to the box-loader, while Hispanic workers perched above the machine on frames rigged out of two-by-fours frantically rake the harvest up the conveyor belts.

This system is just the latest in a series of technological and organizational processes that have transformed "bright" tobacco culture in the past few decades. The most obvious recent change—the death of the warehouse system of leaf marketing—gets a lot of media attention. For a century, the warehouse auctions mediated between agriculture and industry, demonstrating both the links and the divisions between manufacturing and raw material production in the tobacco industry. The colorful ritual is now giving way to direct contracts between grower and buyer, often penned before the farmer sets the seedlings in the field. Yet the demise of the warehouses obscures more important but subtler changes in agricultural production. The bright tobacco culture that flourished on the North Carolina-Virginia border, eventually spreading south into parts of South Carolina, Georgia, and Florida, was once characterized by arduous, skilled labor, but since World War II agricultural mechanization has dramatically changed

bright tobacco agriculture, especially its uses of land and labor. Technological change, however, is both the cause and the effect of social and economic transformations. The recent mechanization of bright tobacco agriculture provides a vivid illustration of how technological and social processes work together to change each other.[1]

The box-loading machine appears at the twelfth stop on the tobacco tour, which lasts two days and extends over dozens of farms and agricultural experiment stations in six counties. Sponsored by various departments at North Carolina State University (including plant pathology, crop science, entomology, and biological and agricultural engineering), the tour brings together different sectors of the tobacco industry: growers and buyers, chemical salesmen and global competitors, academics and the public. For many, it's an opportunity to visit with old friends, examine new technology, and eyeball this year's crop. N.C. State sponsors the tour to demonstrate its extension work and to exhibit the fieldwork of agricultural research stations. Months of experimentation have produced information about varietal disease resistance, insecticides, and fungicides. Tip studies have attempted to wrest more value from the topmost leaves of the plant. The

For a century, tobacco was sold to manufacturers in lively warehouse auctions. The death of that system is just one of the major changes that the tobacco industry has undergone in recent years. Tobacco warehouse interiors, courtesy of the North Carolina Collection in Wilson Library (above) and the Southern Historical Collection (below) at the The University of North Carolina at Chapel Hill.

tour stops at field after field of tobacco where the rows bear placards that say what was done to them. We walk into the fields to finger the leaves and make our own judgments: Did this chemical control the mosaic virus and, in this year's drought, prevent stunting? What resistance do different varieties show to the different kinds of black shank disease? When did budworms take over this field?

I'm here because I'm writing a dissertation at the University of North Carolina about the history of bright tobacco. My first forays into research raised some serious technical questions: for example, Nannie May Tilley, bright tobacco's most esteemed historian, implied in *The Bright-Tobacco Industry* (1948) that only one variety of tobacco existed between 1865 and 1935, the period I study, while other evidence indicates that different regions, and even sometimes distinct counties or farms, produced different kinds of tobacco for particular purposes and unique markets. Which was it? One variety or many? I needed to know, and I also wanted to establish relationships with scientists who could answer such questions as they arose. So I went on-line and found an agronomist at N.C. State who teaches a course every spring on flue-cured tobacco production. I sent this Philip Morris Professor of Crop Science an email explaining my interest and asking for clarification on historical varieties. He told me what he knew, and forwarded my question to a geneticist and fellow member of "the tobacco faculty" at State. Before long, the tobacco breeder had dug up and mailed me the 1936 article that could answer my question.[2]

Technological innovations, such as the box-loading machine, have considerably altered the way bright tobacco is grown and processed. Photograph courtesy of the author.

The tobacco faculty at State answered my question with the air of men who count public service as a major component of their jobs, men who assume reflexively that everyone who asks for professional help deserves every piece of it they can give. The geneticist mentioned the tour and suggested I come along if I had any interest. People drive their own cars, so I could join and leave the tour at any time; the itinerary was on the web and the trip was free. Did I have any interest? Did I? *Did I?* I did not want to write for ten years about tobacco without ever having seen a field of the stuff. And I wanted to meet tobacco people. So I went. Rather than drive across the state to join the tour at its beginning at 7:00 a.m., I picked it up during lunchtime of the first day, at the Central Crops Research Station, where the public is always welcome.[3]

The university conveys the impression that it strives to serve the public, which somehow includes me. During the tour, this attitude of public service came to seem natural, the usual outcome of that commingling of academia, industry, and the state that assists American agriculture, which I've begun to call "big agricultural science." This system of interconnected government, university, and industrial dollars — this single body composed of distinct parts, personnel, and knowledge — developed in the later nineteenth century with the founding of the U.S. Department of Agriculture and its counterparts in state governments, and the establishment of federal funding for agricultural and technical colleges in every state. Big agricultural science shares many of the characteristics of the postwar

"Did I have any interest? Did I? Did I? I hoped to prevent the situation in which I write for ten years about tobacco without ever having seen a field of the stuff." Photograph courtesy of the author.

"big science" that takes place in academic laboratories, funded by government grants, and staffed with research fellows sponsored by defense industry corporations. But long before the atomic bomb brought government dollars into university physics labs, the state of North Carolina had a chemist in Chapel Hill using the university's Chemical Laboratory to analyze fertilizers. That was 1877, and from the first the job requirements emphasized spreading the results to farmers so they would know what they were getting for their money.[4]

Fertilizers were a big help in establishing North Carolina's bright tobacco agriculture, a unique combination of environmental effects and cultivation techniques that has brought the state undisputed and long-standing preeminence in tobacco leaf production. Even today the state produces more tobacco than any other in the union. North Carolina's current population of 8 million includes 12,095 families that grow tobacco. The tobacco industry employs another 255,000 of her citizens; altogether, nearly 32 North Carolinians in every 1000 make a living, one way or another, from tobacco. In contrast, the state's plum example of Sunbelt development, the Research Triangle Park, employs only 6 out of every 1,000 people in the state—and workers whose degrees come from North Carolina universities fill only a quarter of these high-tech jobs. Tobacco agriculture alone generates about $722.5 million in income—with ten times that economic impact—in this state alone. As is typical in big science, the government and the manufacturing side of the tobacco industry together help support NC State. Academia, in turn, contributes its faculty and expertise directly to farmers in the form of agricultural extension work. And the Tobacco Tour exists to demonstrate some of the benefits that trickle down from that work.[5]

After lunch on the first day of the tour, the extension agent blows his horn to signal time to move on to the next stop. The visitors amble back to their cars and trucks and vans and ease them into a single file. I ease in with them, edging into the motorcade for a high-speed chase down country lanes, state roads, and interstates. These people drive like maniacs. We fly by soybeans but slow down to admire pretty fields of tobacco. In a motorcade of at least sixty vehicles this stop-and-go style can create some serious gaps in the line. The state supports our passage, stationing policemen at intersections who let us run red lights, with hand-offs among the Person, Granville, Duplin, and Wilson county cops as we cross jurisdictions. It works like a funeral on the way to the gravesite. And just like a wake, we have our lights on. Sometimes the police mistake a gap for the end of the line, and when the convoy gets on I-95, we have no chance of sticking together. But enough state vans carry enough people who know where to go, and everyone eventually arrives at every farm, field, and station.

Twenty-five minutes down the pike, we all pull over on the side of a country road and park, two and three deep in the grass beside the asphalt, for a demonstration called "Budworm Threshold." We spill out of our cars with cameras and

Today, almost 32 of every 1000 North Carolinians make a living from tobacco—more than five times the number employed by the state's high-profile Research Triangle Park. The crop has been a mainstay of the state's economy for over a century. Workers hanging tobacco in a Kinston stemming and drying plant in 1935, courtesy of the North Carolina Collection in Wilson Library at The University of North Carolina at Chapel Hill.

booklets of experimental data, and suddenly I'm in my first tobacco field. This field is a site of cooperative extension, where different parts of the industry work together with one purpose, where farmers plant their fields and graduate students perform experiments, first implanting budworms "right down into the bud, just like a real infestation," then visiting and revisiting their plants. Unfortunately, a hailstorm destroyed this crop a few days ago, so it lacks the order I expect of farms—not to mention experiments. Some plants have flowers; some do not, and crumpled leaves tilt from their broken stalks between the rows. The entomologist running this stop, Professor P. Sterling Southern, explains the situation through a cordless public address system. The insurance company has declared the crop a 90 percent loss. The entomologist suggests that the farmer, a model of cooperative experimentation who does just what the faculty tells him to do, hasn't been living right. The act of God came too late to change the itinerary but not before graduate students had collected some useful data on rates of budworm proliferation. These data have been collected in the tour booklet, which folks consult as they move through the pitiful hail-hammered field.

As we walk along, I ask questions of the air: Why have some plants flowered and others not? Miraculously, the man beside me answers. He points out that some of the plants had probably not flowered until the hail "stressed them out. Plants under stress try to reproduce, pop up a bunch of flowers." The plants without flowers had already been topped. This means that the flowers had been chopped off and the stump treated with a chemical that prevents the most extravagant growth of the suckers, secondary growths that sprout after flowering. The man pulls aside the suckers so I can see the blackened flower stump. I recognize the plant's parts from books, but nothing had prepared me for its magnificent height, nearly as tall as I am. And now I know for the first time that the flowers are kind of pink.

Later I learn from a professor emeritus that the tobacco faculty doesn't like to make such a poor show as this hail-beaten field to buyers and competitors. Maybe two dozen of the hundred-odd folks on the tour either head large agricultural concerns abroad or represent foreign tobacco industries: Brazil, Croatia, China, the Philippines. The Americans on the tour come mostly from the industry; only a few growers show up outside their own counties. Most people on the tour are men and very helpful. I'm impressed that my presence doesn't faze them at all. I'm a fat midwestern Jew, wearing my usual black drapery, and my wild, graying-black curly hair sticks up in the heat and humidity of the tour. My face would look at home in Prague in 1865, but not in North Carolina at that time, and the hot southern sun flushes my ethnic features a deep red. I like to think my people have been urban for millennia. But if the tobacco people find me odd, they hide it well. Perhaps behind their smooth, supple, inscrutable southern personas they have raised their eyebrows, but their faces reveal little. Welcome. Here's the answer to your question. Glad you wore comfortable shoes.

TOBACCO'S PAST

Tobacco has been grown for profit in the world marketplace since Europeans settled at Jamestown; cultivation for export underwrote many English colonies. The plant has played a crucial role in some of the most important processes in American history, from the foundations of slavery to the coming of the American Revolution, from the rise of big business to the formation of the welfare state. One of the first things Europeans noticed about the New World was how much its natives smoked. The designers of the Capitol Building in Washington acknowledged the significance of the plant by working it into the capitals of columns, lending a homegrown style to the classical Corinthian orders that house the national legislative works. At one time, tobacco grew all across the nation, from the Carolinas to Connecticut, from Virginia to Kentucky. But the myriad varieties of the plant, as I eventually learned with the help of the tobacco faculty,

"These people drive like maniacs. We fly by soybeans but slow down to admire pretty fields of tobacco."
Scenes from the 2002 Tobacco Tour, courtesy of the author.

really represent only a very few genetically distinct types. The plant's sensitivity to cultural factors means that the specific cultivation methods that developed in different regions resulted in unique products, many more types of tobacco for sale than the few natural varieties can account for.[6]

The Tobacco Tour focuses on North Carolina's characteristic product, the bright, or flue-cured, tobacco that emerged before the Civil War. For decades bright tobacco found its market as mere packaging, a lemony-yellow wrapper for twists of the dark, rich plug tobacco. As the twentieth century approached, however, mild flue-cured tobacco became the perfect raw material for the fashionable inhalable cigarettes that propelled the booming tobacco industry. Bright tobacco becomes light and mild not simply because it is flue-cured, but because of a particular set of environmental, cultural, and technological conditions. The Orinoco variety, the same kind that colonists grew at Jamestown, provided the seeds of the original bright leaf, but it sprang up light and mild as desired only on poor soil: gray and sandy, full of silicates, a dusty earth that starves the tobacco of the nutrients that make its leaves dark and bitter. Many of the techniques used to grow the bright leaf, however, differed little from those of its cousins: all commercially grown tobacco gets sown in seedbeds, then transplanted into the fields. All varieties require topping and suckering. There, however, the similarity ends. Distinctive methods of harvesting and curing the leaf make bright tobacco really become bright.[7]

The venerable Nannie May Tilley has handed down the following Genesis legend of the leaf: Stephen, a slave blacksmith on Abisha Slade's Caswell County plantation, in North Carolina near the Virginia border, was curing a barn of tobacco by an open-fire method. He fell asleep and let the rain extinguish his curing fires. When he woke, he corrected his mistake by stoking the fire high with charcoal, filling the barn with a sudden intense heat. When opened a few days later, the barn contained "six hundred pounds of the brightest yellow tobacco ever seen." From that point on, according to Tilley, the technologies of bright tobacco production developed directly, in a straightforward fashion. Further experimentation established when and how much to vary the temperature, and what material to burn in the fire. Before long, farmers protected the leaves from smoke and controlled the flow of heat through the barn by containing it in ducts, or "flues," lining the floor of the curing barn. At first the barns had stone flues, but eventually metal ductwork proved most popular. Landowners erected thousands of these flue-lined curing barns on the tiny parcels they rented to families, often simply for shares of the crop.[8]

The peculiar methods of harvesting bright tobacco, historians inform us, merely refined the methods born in Stephen's fire. In order to ensure an even color, leaves of the same ripeness were cured in the same barn. Tobacco ripens from the bottom up, at least in the latitudes of Virginia and North Carolina.

The turn-of-the-century period saw a boom in the tobacco industry, sparked by the new popularity of cigarettes. Duke of Durham, pictured here in 1895, was one of the boom's greatest beneficiaries. Photograph courtesy of the North Carolina Collection in Wilson Library at The University of North Carolina at Chapel Hill.

Therefore the bright leaf harvest became a laborious process known as priming, in which men went through the fields taking only the ripe, or prime, leaves, beginning at the bottom and, over the course of several weeks, continuing up the stalk. After harvesting, the leaves went by sled to the curing barns, where women tied or looped them onto sticks in bunches. Children carried the sticks into the curing barns and suspended them from the lower tiers. At the end of the day, on returning from the fields, the men would hang the sticks from the tops of the barns and close the doors for the week-long manipulation of temperature that curing required. After curing, the leaves still needed grading for sale, a process that could continue on into the next crop year. The long marketing season, or maybe just the endless hard work, gave tobacco the nickname "the thirteen-month crop."[9]

I study the history of technology, which means that I pay particular attention to these techniques—how they developed and what that might mean. I find myself distrusting this story of linear progress toward ever more efficient production methods. I notice that priming served social and economic purposes as much as productivity requirements. For example, rotating the workforce through the fields on a weekly basis involved larger units of labor than individual households could supply. The arrangement relied on extended families and neighbor groups and, by incorporating traditional household labor relations, made good use of every man, woman, and child, every day of the harvest. Priming also performed valuable functions for landlords and the tobacco industry. Because tobacco grades relate to where the leaf grew on the stalk, priming roughly graded the leaf before curing. Easier grading got the crop to market more quickly after the harvest, which freed tenants sooner from the crop. Shorter marketing seasons, too, allowed the industry's leaf buyers to work more than one area, moving north with the harvest, saving skilled labor costs. Priming was not only laborious, it was a complicated structure, a technological system that blurred the line between the natural requirements of the crop and the social norms of the tobacco culture.[10]

While I am coming to understand how many purposes priming served, I don't yet know who introduced the technique, or when and why, or how the method took hold and spread—but I'm hot on the trail. I want to understand how and why that system took shape because technology sets the limits of the possible. The technological system of harvest and curing meant that farms stayed small, and the New Deal made sure they stayed that way. In order to preserve a living for farm families by keeping prices paid for farm goods above the cost of growing them, Franklin D. Roosevelt's Agricultural Adjustment Administration began to control commodity production in the 1930s. In the case of flue-cured tobacco, the federal government's production-control and price-support system took the form of allotments: assigned limits on the amount of land on which tobacco could be grown. Federal allotments averaged around five acres. The economic arrangements of sharecropping and tenancy combined with the laborious methods of harvesting and curing to inspire federal policies that worked to keep farm operations small, arduous, and reliant on the work of the whole extended family at harvest time to bring the crop to market. Federal policy took its cue from existing land, labor, and technological systems, then locked these systems into place.[11]

THE TOUR CONTINUES

The horn blows, signaling that it's time for the tour to leave the hail-beaten "Budworm Threshold" field, where a stranger helped me spot which plants had already been topped, where I first recognized suckers. The itinerary tells me that we're moving on to a stop called "Precision Nitrogen" that's about forty minutes away, in the next county. As the motorcade flies through the bright belt I begin to recognize the old curing barns. Most have fallen into disuse or now serve other purposes. They have rusting tin-strip roofs and occasionally tin siding, though most have walls of wood. Foliage cloaks the abandoned structures. Framed windows down by the ground show where the furnace, half inside the barn and half outside for stoking, once joined the metal flues. Many of the old barns stand in pairs, I now see, with a roof between them. Some farmers have turned these barns to other uses; others park machines under the roofs between paired barns. But most lie in ruins. They line the country roads, markers of the tiny parcels landowners once rented out to farmers. While a few barns have found new uses as storage or outbuildings, most deteriorate into rubble. Few serve any useful purpose, but they are not so old as to be rare.

The mass-produced modern barns look vaguely like trailers. They began to replace the old barns in the 1960s—and with the barns went the extended family labor rotation system, the looping work of women, the distinctive rhythms of curing. Nowadays, the leaves get cured in wire boxes that fit precisely into the prefabricated metal curing barns, with gauges and dials to determine and adjust the temperature. The shift to bulk curing accompanied the mechanization of topping and suckering, a tiny but critical change in the growing process. In the sum-

After the leaves had been harvested, they were transported to curing barns, where women looped them onto sticks. Next, the bunches of leaves would be hung inside the barns for the week-long curing process. Looping tobacco in the 1930s, courtesy of the North Carolina Collection in Wilson Library at The University of North Carolina at Chapel Hill.

mers before World War II, removing flowering tops and then suckers were tasks done by hand. With machines and chemicals doing the work, labor needs largely disappeared between the setting out of seedlings and the harvest. The change made most summer work unnecessary. People without jobs in agriculture moved to cities and industries north or south, to public work in mill and mine, leaving the fields even less labor at harvest time. Priming served too many other important purposes to disappear, however, and any machine had to reproduce the technique in order to work. In 1971 agricultural engineers at N.C. State, sponsored by R. J. Reynolds, patented a harvesting machine that pulled leaves only from the ripest part of the stalk.[12]

As it turns out, the Precision Nitrogen stop has a harvesting machine on display, a Powell Manufacturing model equipped with a global positioning system. The GPS helps farmers and faculty match nitrogen levels in every square inch of the soil to fertilizer application, then correlate these data to yield maps, created by scales on the harvester that weigh the leaves as they drop into the boxes. This "precision farming" attempts to reduce fertilizer runoff into the state's waterways. I've spent long hours reading the patents for this and other harvesters, and

Priming required more labor than most households possessed, and so tobacco farmers such as these in the 1920s called on extended families and neighbors to help with the harvest. Photograph courtesy of the North Carolina Collection in Wilson Library at The University of North Carolina at Chapel Hill.

so I lean into it, fondle and photograph its rubbery defoliators. I'm so excited that I'm chatting about harvester design with the stranger beside me. We talk about when the defoliators are replaced with cutting bars. "After two, maybe three primings," he tells me, because the tobacco stalk gets more limber higher up, requiring a different kind of edge to remove the stringy leaf. The fellow puffs his pipe and then gives me his card. He's a manager in Philip Morris's leaf department. I ask him if I can call him and ask questions, maybe sit down sometime and talk about tobacco. He says yes, and we agree that I should wait until the harvest is done for the year.

Soon enough, the horn blows. One more stop—the eighth of the day—illustrates tests of systemic insecticide. Then we all retire to a complex in Rocky Mount, where a Holiday Inn, a Comfort Inn, and an Outback Steakhouse cradle a convention center that, I suspect, sees a lot of tobacco business. A few hours later the tour reconvenes for an hors d'oeuvres and cash-bar reception in the sports bar of the Holiday Inn. I arrive fairly early and join a table. As soon as I explain my presence, people begin to talk about the old ways. They give me their cards that bear the logos of chemical-pharmaceutical companies and machine manufacturers, and more Philip Morris and N.C. State. As they share stories, I begin to realize that these are tobacco people, farm children who grew up into scientists or salesmen. The men tell stories about how it was when they were boys. We chat about how their worlds have changed. We talk about the bulk barns and the harvesting machines, and when and why they displaced old arrangements for priming and curing. We trade theories. I'm buying beers and bumming cigarettes. People think of other folks I should contact. I scribble names on the backs of the cards that begin to fill my wallet.

They smoke less than I had imagined. I assumed the tobacco industry would be thick with smokers, but the proportion of smokers in the room seems similar to that of any convention at a hotel bar. Perhaps a third of the people in the room smoke cigarettes, pipes, or cigars, though the percentage increases as the evening lengthens. After eleven o'clock, of course, the people who remain will tend more and more toward the hard-core, folks willing to stay up all night drinking despite the fact that the caravan will pull out of the parking lot at seven the next morning. The two bartenders keep plenty busy. Old friends greet each other, mingle into fluid knots, and table-hop around the room. Some buddies link their arms around each other's shoulders and begin to sing. I had expected Big Tobacco to be wary of outsiders, paranoid about its business. Instead, I find its representatives forming this community, offering me hospitality, friendly and eager to share what they know. All the different limbs of the industry are here tonight, displaying the way they fit together. Tobacco people come out of tobacco agriculture and resemble the tobacco faculty in all its unruffled agreeable willingness to help me out.

"The old ways [above] were about quality, now [below] it's mostly quantity. If I even stepped on a leaf of tobacco as a boy I'd get a whuppin'. Now the leaves are all beat to hell." Old and new, courtesy of the North Carolina Collection in Wilson Library at The University of North Carolina at Chapel Hill and courtesy of the author respectively.

A good old boy named Stan buys me drinks and offers me lots of useful advice. He has an easy good humor that must come in handy in his job selling chemicals, and he also shares the tobacco folk's intimate knowledge of the plant. He tells me to visit the counties where bright culture first developed if I want to see older processes still in use. A representative of Powell Manufacturing supports this statement. He has trouble selling machines there. "They say it's the lay of the land, or whatever. They want me to prove that the harvester works. I say, prove it? We've sold these systems all over the bright belt. We know they work. You do too." But Stan counters that these people pursue the old ways for good reasons, and the lay of the land is one of them. "Plus they produce a boutique leaf, and there'll always be a market for that product. The old ways were about quality, now it's mostly quantity. If I even stepped on a leaf of tobacco as a boy I'd get a whuppin. Now the leaves are all beat to hell. Not all. Certainly not all. But quantity matters now, and it'll matter more with the buy-out coming."

"Some people are growing who never did before, just to get on that list for when the buy-out comes." I have willingly asked stupid questions and received patient, enlightening answers all day and into the evening, and eventually I ask, what do you mean when you talk about the buy-out? It turns out that they mean the proposed dismantling of the entire price-support and production-control system the federal government has enforced, with some tinkering, since the New Deal. Stan thinks this is a good thing. "We'll get rid of the worst growers, maybe to the tenth or fifteenth, maybe, percentile. That won't destroy the livelihood of those that do well." A pale-lashed agronomist—from a purchasing company whose logo resembles a yin-and-yang symbol, but made of two tobacco leaves— nods his assent. The agronomist wants to know, though, if the remaining growers will be able to produce enough leaf, given the opportunity, to meet the demands of manufacturers in the absence of production controls. "That's the big number-one black hole question," Stan admits. "In two-three years, sure, they can grow whatever's wanted. But in the meantime? And how will they recapture that market when they can finally grow the product? When we're talkin' recapture . . ." he pauses, and considers, mouth open, "things get tougher."

They know their world is dying, but they are southern and so prefer mourning to complaining. They make their living out of a deeply unpopular consumer product. They study it scientifically, or design machines to cultivate it, sell fertilizer to its farmers, test its composition, roll it into paper, and sell it around the world. No one here seems into killing people to rack up the profits. At one of the day's stops, an extension agent admitted ruefully, good-naturedly into the microphone that tobacco isn't a very attractive subject for graduate study these days. The farmwife who offered me lunch told me she hopes her children don't smoke. This Big Tobacco doesn't resemble cancer-land or faceless corporate America. These people with very different jobs, but who know each other and know the same things, make a world that feels comfortably collegial, not unlike an academic conference. They treat me so kindly, I think, because they know people must question me about my research subject with the same distrust they feel for the tobacco industry. I didn't bring my notebook, and later someone tells me that's good: if I'd carried a notebook people would have thought I was a lawyer. "It doesn't matter for which side. A lawyer's a lawyer."

The long-term effects of smoking on human health began to receive the sustained attention of medical experiments in the 1950s, and the Surgeon General's first report on *Smoking and Health* appeared in 1964. U.S. tobacco consumption has declined ever since. Nowadays the public seems willing to consider smoking at least as much a danger to the commonweal as to the individual. The medical costs of dying young appear to many to ring a heavier charge on the public purse than do the myriad ills of old age. Movies and television portray Big Tobacco as evil personified, the devil, the beast. Like all animals, however, the beast is composed of parts that resemble one another not at all. Think about it: What American smiles on a farm's foreclosure? Even a tobacco farm? Especially a tobacco farm, a family farm by definition and law for half a century, "the single remaining example of the Jeffersonian ideal, a small-farm yeomanry"? Politicians have spent decades trying to distinguish between smoking issues and farm subsidies, indus-

People who work in various aspects of the tobacco industry form a collegial community—but they realize that due to public health awareness and other industry pressures their world is dying. Photograph from the 2002 Tobacco Tour, courtesy of the author.

try and agriculture, hoping to cut apart for policy purposes a living world whose parts function together not only at the warehouse, but also in its population and personnel—the farmers, buyers, scientists, executives.[13]

"These are farm people," the fellow from Powell Manufacturing told me at the reception, warning me that the tour starts early. "They're probably up at 4:30 or 5:00, waiting for the day to get started." Official start-up time is 7:00 a.m., so I set the hotel's digital alarm for 5:30. When I wake up I make a bit of coffee, shower, and dress, and slather on the sunscreen—not neglecting, today, the back of my neck. By 6:30 the line of cars has begun to form, stretching between the two hotels. I hurry downstairs, check out, get in my car, and get in line. People aren't very talkative. Most stay in their cars, ready for the day to start. Breakfast, supplied I think by R. J. Reynolds, will be served at the experiment station that is our first stop. It's time to check out how the different varieties of tobacco are more or less resistant to the two separate kinds of Black Shank disease. The horn blows. The caravan gets rolling. The young extension agent holds up the same sign as yesterday: "Turn your lights on!"

The first stop consists of several different events and locations. Breakfast beckons from broad tables: biscuits with sausage inside, piping hot and wrapped in tinfoil, Krispy Kreme doughnuts, coffee, and juice. I sip coffee and, like everyone

The 2002 Tobacco Tour's attendees pored over countless rows of tobacco. Courtesy of the author.

The death of the warehouse system means an end to the busy season for many small towns. Tobacco warehouse district in Louisville, Kentucky, in the early twentieth century, courtesy of the North Carolina Collection in Wilson Library at The University of North Carolina at Chapel Hill.

else, stare dully out at the fields. At this first stop, an older man approaches me. "Are you the one writing the dissertation?" he asks. I allow that I am. He introduces himself—Bill Collins—and tells me that he has retired from the tobacco faculty at State, that he used to teach the course in flue-cured tobacco production, and that he wrote the textbook used in the class. The new professors still assign his book, which means that, in important ways, he still teaches the class and will continue to do so probably after his death. Bill wants to know, do I want a copy? If so, will I give him my contact information? I say I'd be very interested, that I had noted the course on the university website and had thought about buying its textbooks from the bookstore in the spring. Then he recalls that he has a copy with him—"in my case"—and will get it for me at the next stop—"to save the postage."

At the next stop I'm staring at rows of tobacco involved in a tip study. Bill finds me, and we walk together—"if you'll come with me"—up the line of cars. When we find his, he opens the trunk and jerks around the suitcases inside, opening one and feeling around inside its extremely orderly contents. With a grunt, he finds the book. He takes out a pen and licks it, then discovers he's already signed the book, a hefty hardcover. "We didn't make any notes," he declares contritely, "just wrote it out of our heads." I try to convey how useful it will be for me—a fine reference for things like nematodes and barn rot—but he tells me, "It has value. If you don't want it, send it to this address," showing me the order form bound into the back pages of the book. "Shipping ought to cost you around a dollar-fifty." I tell him I have no intention of losing this book. I thank him, but I don't think I've managed to express how glad I am to have the gift. He glowers a bit, considering.

Two stops later, Bill returns to my side. He's beginning to tell me some of his story. His grandparents were tenants—"white tenants, of course"—and his parents were landlords who had tenants of their own. He doesn't know how the next generation acquired land to rent to others. His mother and father used to fight about where the tenant children belonged, in the fields or in school. His mother won, so many of his family's tenants received at least a ninth-grade education. "Of course we had separate schools for black and white then, and they were older than me, so I don't know how they all did, but I know some thrived and prospered." One may have become a bookkeeper, he thinks; as far as he knows, none stayed on the land. Farm tenancy and sharecropping thrived on the small bright-tobacco farms, but mechanization required larger parcels. The new, bulk-curing barns stand in paired ranks of ten or more, serving much bigger farms than the old ones did. The New Deal allotments rarely surpassed ten acres, but Bill tells me that the average acreage most farms hold in tobacco nowadays numbers more like eighty.

The designers of the first harvesting machines planned for farmers to break even at somewhere between about forty and fifty acres. Mechanization could not pay in the small-scale units that production methods had originally demanded and that the federal government later enforced. The new machines for topping, suckering, harvesting, and curing would have been useless without policy changes that allowed farmers—those with substantial resources—to change their uses of land, labor, and capital. Shifts in land-use began early in the 1960s, when the government first started letting farmers lease one another's allotments. Consolidating the properties once rented to numerous tenants, landowners accumulated allotments and increased the scale of their farm operations. The technological momentum that built from the shift to bulk curing and the mechanization of topping and suckering could not by itself account for the transition to mechanized harvesting. The political system had to change for the technology to work. Changes in one segment of the industry sped changes elsewhere: adjustments in land-use, shifts in labor timing and availability, and the development of new technologies all worked together to transform tobacco agriculture.[14]

Until just about last year, farmers brought their tobacco to warehouses to sell

Equipment primes the leaves and a modified school bus delivers them to the box loader at this stop on the 2002 Tobacco Tour (above). Harvesting equipment has changed a great deal since the 1920s (below). Photographs courtesy of the author and courtesy of the North Carolina Collection in Wilson Library at The University of North Carolina at Chapel Hill respectively.

at auction. The crop had not come to market precisely graded and tied into hands for a generation or more. The change to bulk-cured, loose-leaf marketing was one part of the transformations in technology and society that produced the mechanized harvest, but it changed little about the relationships between buyers and sellers, industry and agriculture. The demise of the warehouse system promises the same kind of surface shift created earlier by changes in marketing. The dozens of small towns that sprang up around the warehouses will see no busy season, but the structural relationships remain the same. "Used to be a good old boy thing," Stan the chemical salesman had told me drunkenly the night before. "Now it's all in writing. Did you hear the extension agents say, for the first time we have to be consumer-conscious, for the first time we're making a product for consumer demand?" I didn't hear that; it must have happened during a morning stop that I missed. When I asked him how the marketing would take place without the warehouses, he told me, "It's a good old boy thing. They know who to go to for what they want."

The two stops right before lunch present a study in contrasts, a moment of transition from one system of tobacco production to another. First we visit a site where the farmer mustered NC State to help him fight what he calls "the worst case of tobacco mosaic virus ever seen in the county." He tearfully introduces his wife, mother, and children. Two dogs tied to the front porch, each with two different-colored eyes, bark happily at the line of cars as we caravan onto the farm. The whole operation looks like maybe fifty acres, and the sagging wooden buildings need paint. Yet the farmer uses bulk barns and harvesting machines and probably just his family's labor. The trip here took longer than expected, so we dash off almost as soon as we arrive, in a hurry to get to our lunch stop, which takes place on the largest family farm I've ever seen. Around five substantial greenhouses run broad immaculate drives of sparkling, white quartz gravel. We lunch at long tables in the hangar-like equipment shed, hear speeches, and applaud the fertilizer company that has paid for our meal. Then we all troop down to the curing barns to get a close look at the brand-new prototype box-loading machine.

The greenhouses apparently give this farmer a head start on the season. Despite the fact that most of the plants along the tour have not yet even flowered, this farm has the harvest going in full swing. Giant machines prime the leaves, and modified school buses accept the machine-plucked leaves and carry them to the box loader. The cut-down back of the bus, a conveyor belt with walls, unloads a bus-sized volume of leaf onto the conveyor belts of the box loader. The belts carry the brown-green leaves high and then drop them onto another belt, fluffing and separating the foliage. From there the leaves drop again, into a chute that carries them twenty feet up to where a claw rocking in three dimensions will blow them evenly into the wire box in which they will cure. The whole elaborate process exists to ensure the even distribution of heat to cure the leaves to a consistent color. New systems made of metal, rubber, and gasoline replace hand priming, hand looping, and the temperature adjustments of curing. It still requires a bit of human aid, mostly to drive the primers and the buses. And workers are stationed around the box loader's conveyor belts, three above and three at the back, to aid the mechanical fluffing.

But the box-loading machine represents the moment when the system of mechanized agricultural tobacco production reaches for its completion. This harvest has been fifty years growing. The process that began with mechanical topping and chemical suckering in the 1950s progressed with great strides in the 1960s with the acceptance of bulk-cured leaves and the beginning of allotment leasing. It reached its climax a decade later in the harvesting machine. The box loader is the next stage, the denouement, as machines begin to replace humans even at the in-between stages of the agricultural process: between the machine harvest and the machine curing, the box loader fills the gap. Similarly, the direct contract replaces the auctioneer. While the completion of mechanization has received less notice in recent years than the demise of the warehouses, the less celebrated change is actually the more dramatic. Now so few people work the land that, someone tells me, the Chinese tourists in his van accused him of sending ahead to get the workers out of the fields.

At the end of the box loader, I find the professor who invited me on the tour. "It's a long way from Nannie May Tilley's day," he says to me, and I agree. There are two more stops this afternoon, another tip study and one cooperative exten-

"The horn blows. It's time to move on." Photograph courtesy of the author.

sion site with a resistance-to-wilt experiment. Both fields promise to be more rows of tobacco plants with placards in front of them—not very exciting except perhaps for the manufacturers of wilt-prevention chemicals—and I'm running out of gas besides. I tell the professor that I'm going to leave the tour now, and thank him for his hospitality and his willing help. We shake hands. We watch the machine at work, as yet imperfectly. Human hands, immigrant hands, help the conveyor belts get the leaves off the school bus and up onto the machine, and other hands fluff the greenery as it goes up the chute to the pivoting head that will blow the leaves evenly into the mesh box. It's a beautiful sight, as human effort and engineering usually are, but it's also a sad one for those nostalgic for America's rural past: as sad as any shuttered warehouse and, in the end, more typical and representative of the recent changes the bright tobacco culture has seen.

The horn blows. It's time to move on.

NOTES

I thank Peter A. Coclanis, Paul Quigley, and the anonymous readers for *Southern Cultures* for their valuable comments and helpful suggestions.

1. For examples of publicity about the death of the warehouse system, see *Washington Post*, 25 March 2001, T01, and 11 August 2001, A03.

2. Nannie May Tilley, *The Bright Tobacco Industry, 1860–1929* (University of North Carolina Press, 1948), 112–17; J. B. Killebrew, "Tobacco Culture," in *Report on the Productions of Agriculture as Returned at the Tenth Census (June 1, 1880), Embracing General Statistics and Monographs on Cereal Production, Flour-Milling, Tobacco Culture, Manufacture and Movement of Tobacco, Meat Production* (U.S. Government Printing Office, 1883), 704–05; W. W. Garner, H. A. Allard, and E. E. Clayton, "Superior Germ Plasm in Tobacco," U.S. Department of Agriculture, *Yearbook*, 1936 (U.S. Government Printing Office, 1937), 785–830.

3. http://www.ncagr.com/research/ccrs.htm, 2 April 2003; 2003 tour information is available at http://www.cals.ncsu.edu/plantpath/ExtensionPro/tobacco_tour.html, 2 April 2003.

4. North Carolina Agricultural Experiment Station, *Annual Report for 1879* (The Observer, State Printer and Binder, 1879), 8–11.

5. http://www.agr.state.nc.us/markets/commodity/horticul/tobacco/, 2 April 2003; http://quickfacts.census.gov/qfd/states/37000.html, 2 April 2003; http://www.rtp.org/rtpfacts/factsheet.html, 2 April 2003; http://www.rtp.org/rtpfacts/bydegree1.html, 2 April 2003.

6. An excellent popular history of tobacco is Iain Gately, *Tobacco: The Story of How Tobacco Seduced the World* (Grove Press, 2001). For tobacco's role in the historical processes mentioned, see, for example, Allan Kulikoff, *Tobacco and Slaves: The Development of Southern Cultures in the Chesapeake, 1680–1800* (University of North Carolina Press, 1986); T.H. Breen, *Tobacco Culture: The Mentality of the Great Tidewater Planters on the Eve of Revolution* (Princeton University Press, 1985); Alfred D. Chandler Jr., *The Visible Hand: The Managerial Revolution in American Business* (Harvard University Press, 1977); and Anthony J. Badger, *Prosperity Road: The New Deal, Tobacco, and North Carolina* (University of North Carolina Press, 1980). For Washington's architecture, see William C. Allen, *History of the United States Capitol: A Chronicle of Design, Construction, and Politics* (U.S. Government Printing Office, 2001), 113, 238–41, 319.

7. Garner et al., "Superior Germ Plasm," 786; Liz Mandrell, "Lilies of the Field: A Tobacco Family Sows a New Crop," *Cincinnati Magazine*, June 2002.

8. Tilley, *Bright Tobacco Industry*, 24–32; Pete Daniel, *Breaking the Land: The Transformation of Cotton, Tobacco, and Rice Cultures since 1880* (University of Illinois Press, 1985), 23–31.

9. Tilley, *Bright Tobacco Industry*, 59, 79–82; Daniel, *Breaking the Land*, 23–31.

10. Interview with Waltz Maynor, 12 March 2002, in the possession of the author.

11. Tilley, *Bright Tobacco Industry*, 24; Daniel, *Breaking the Land,* 23–31.

12. Daniel, *Breaking the Land,* 262–66.

13. William R. Finger, introduction to *The Tobacco Industry in Transition: Policies for the 1980s* (D. C. Heath and Company, 1981), xi; U.S. Surgeon General's Advisory Committee, *Smoking and Health: Report of the Advisory Committee to the Surgeon General of the Public Health Service* (U.S. Government Printing Office, 1964); http://www.cdc.gov/tobacco/who/usa.htm, 2 April 2003.

14. Daniel, *Breaking the Land,* 263–65.

Enough About the Disappearing South
What About the Disappearing Southerner?

by Larry J. Griffin and Ashley B. Thompson

*P*rofound transformations in the South since the 1960s have led many observers to sound the region's death knell. Distinctive and exceptional no longer, they say, the region has been disappearing, vanishing, shrinking, and converging with mainstream America for decades, a victim of relentless incorporation into mass society. In a brief but stark *Time* magazine essay published in 1990, Hodding Carter III, a former Mississippi newspaper editor transplanted to Washington, D.C., went even further, voicing the judgment that the South was dead: "The South as South, a living, ever regenerating mythic land of distinctive personality, is no more. At most it is an artifact lovingly preserved in the museums of culture and the shops of tourist commerce precisely because it is so hard to find in the vital centers of the region's daily life . . . the South is dead. . . . . What is lurching into existence in the South is purely and contemporaneously mainstream American, for better and for worse."[1]

Historian James Cobb reminds us, however, that epitaphs for the region are nothing new: Dixie's demise has been announced since at least the late nineteenth century. Still, those of us who came of age before the civil rights revolution, and those of us who study and teach the South, cannot help being astonished at how different the region is (and, for some, viscerally feels) since, say, 1960. This is not to say that the region is indistinguishable from America—if for no other reason, because its tragic, painful past continues uniquely to evoke commentary, reflection, and condemnation—or that it has solved all of its racial problems. But the South of the 1950s and 1960s—the Jim Crow, culturally insular, economically impoverished, politically retrograde South—*is* dead.[2] Epitaphs for *that* South are indeed in order.

But what, if anything, does all this imply about southern identity, about being a southerner? If the very thing that gives southern identity gravity and salience—a South distinct and genuinely set apart from the rest of the country—is itself disappearing, or, even, no more, are southerners as a group with a distinct, self-declared identity also disappearing, themselves a dying breed?

"The South as South, a living, ever regenerating mythic land of distinctive personality, is no more." Photograph courtesy of the Charleston Convention and Visitor's Bureau.

The answer to this question is not at all obvious. On the one hand, social identity expressed in terms of membership in a distinct group—identity of the sort signified by statements such as "Yes, I am a southerner"—no doubt best flourishes when the distinctive culture with which one identifies is, in Hodding Carter III's words, a "living" reality. On the other hand, identification with the South could, for some, mean little more than the happenstance of residence ("I live in the South, so of course I am a southerner") and thus be little affected by the presumed dissolution of a southern exceptionalism as much moral as cognitive. Of much greater cultural significance is that even in the absence of marked regional distinctiveness, some southerners may continue to identify with the region due to their self-proclaimed membership in what political scientist Benedict Anderson called, in a discussion of nationalism, an "imagined community," by which he means a "fraternity" of "comradeship" in which members "will never know most of their fellow-members, meet them, or even hear of them, yet in the minds of each lives the image of their communion." Southerners of this sort practice what we might call "symbolic southernness."[3] Largely ancestral, honorific, and selectively enacted rather than rooted in the routines of daily life or the attributions of nonsoutherners, "symbolic southernness" need not rest on an actually existing

The Jim Crow, culturally insular, economically impoverished, politically retrograde South—is dead. Epitaphs for that South are indeed in order. Photograph courtesy of the North Carolina Collection in Wilson Library at The University of North Carolina at Chapel Hill.

distinctive South. Indeed, symbolic southerners are able to proclaim their heritage and differentiate themselves from the mass of Americans by grounding their sense of who they are in a mythic place existing mainly in cultural memory—the South as an imagined community—rather than in a "real" space. Southern exceptionalism may be waning, then, but what about southern identity?

The earliest polling data on southern identity comes from a 1971 survey of roughly eleven hundred North Carolinians conducted by sociologists John Shelton Reed and Glen Elder. Then, just at the tail end of the civil rights era, the great majority of respondents, roughly 80 percent (82 percent of whites, 73 percent of African Americans), affirmed their southernness when told "Some people here think of themselves as Southern, others do not" and then explicitly asked, "How about you—would you say you are a Southerner or not?" Though instructive and useful as a benchmark to gauge change over the last thirty years, this poll obviously is not representative of the South as a whole. Reliable information from geographically inclusive samples of southerners about their regional identity exists only since 1991, in a poll administered by the University of North Carolina (UNC), and from broadly representative samples of southerners only since 1992, when the UNC Southern Focus Poll was first fielded.[4]

Until 2000 the Focus Poll was administered twice yearly (in the fall and spring) by telephone to a randomly chosen, representative sample of roughly 700 to 1100 "geographic" southerners, defined by the Poll as inhabitants of the former Confederate states plus Kentucky and Oklahoma, and, until recently, 400 to 500 "nonsoutherners." The 2000 and 2001 polls were administered once, in the spring of each year. The target populations were U.S. adults eighteen years of age or older, residing in houses with telephones. Geographic southerners were always

Are southerners themselves a dying breed? Photograph reproduced from the Collections of the Library of Congress.

over-sampled (relative to their proportions in the nation's population) to insure a large statistical representation in the survey, and the Poll occasionally over-sampled African Americans for the same reason. In the trend analysis reported below, we look only at geographic southerners and combine the fall and spring surveys for years 1992–1999 to smooth away minor intra-year fluctuations.[5] Altogether, about 17,600 geographic southerners were studied in the nineteen polls fielded since 1991.

Each of these polls asked an identically worded question about southern identity phrased quite similarly to the one used by Reed and Elder in their 1971 survey of North Carolinians, "Do you consider yourself to be a Southerner, or not?" Our measure of regional identity should be understood as a gauge of identification *as* a southerner and not necessarily as an indicator of identification *with* other southerners. The former involves categorizing oneself as a member of a regional group, itself understood by Reed as "a reference group, a cognitive entity that people use to orient themselves." The latter, on the other hand, expresses affect, warmth, and empathy toward one's regional group.[6] Responses to the "Do you consider yourself" question, then, are the basis for the comparison to the 1971 survey and for the trend analysis of geographic southerners' identification as regional group members over the period 1991 to 2001.

INDIVIDUAL *subscription request*

Please enter my subscription to *Southern Cultures* at the rate of $28 for four quarterly issues [Add $12 for postage outside the US.] *This price is good until December 31, 2003*

q   My check or money order, payable to THE UNIVERSITY OF NORTH CAROLINA PRESS, is enclosed in an envelope with this card.

q   Please charge my Visa or MasterCard [circle one].

CARD NUMBER _____ EXP. DATE _____

SIGNATURE _____ DAYTIME PHONE _____

NAME _____

ADDRESS _____

_____ ZIP CODE _____

Southern Cultures

For fastest service, please call [919] 966-3561, ext. 256, Monday–Friday between 9:30 a.m. and 4:00 p.m. EST with credit card information or fax your order to [800] 272-6817. You can also send e-mail to uncpress_journals@unc.edu.

INDIVIDUAL *subscription request*

Please enter my subscription to *Southern Cultures* at the rate of $28 for four quarterly issues [Add $12 for postage outside the US.] *This price is good until December 31, 2003*

q   My check or money order, payable to THE UNIVERSITY OF NORTH CAROLINA PRESS, is enclosed in an envelope with this card.

q   Please charge my Visa or MasterCard [circle one].

CARD NUMBER _____ EXP. DATE _____

SIGNATURE _____ DAYTIME PHONE _____

NAME _____

ADDRESS _____

_____ ZIP CODE _____

INDIVIDUAL *subscription request*

Please enter my subscription to *Southern Cultures* at the rate of $28 for four quarterly issues [Add $12 for postage outside the US.] *This price is good until December 31, 2003*

q   My check or money order, payable to THE UNIVERSITY OF NORTH CAROLINA PRESS, is enclosed in an envelope with this card.

q   Please charge my Visa or MasterCard [circle one].

CARD NUMBER _____ EXP. DATE _____

SIGNATURE _____ DAYTIME PHONE _____

NAME _____

ADDRESS _____

_____ ZIP CODE _____

BUSINESS REPLY MAIL
FIRST CLASS MAIL   PERMIT NO. 509   CHAPEL HILL, NC

Postage will be paid by addressee:

The University of North Carolina Press
Journals Fulfillment
Post Office Box 2288
Chapel Hill, NC 27515-2288

BUSINESS REPLY MAIL
FIRST CLASS MAIL   PERMIT NO. 509   CHAPEL HILL, NC

Postage will be paid by addressee:

The University of North Carolina Press
Journals Fulfillment
Post Office Box 2288
Chapel Hill, NC 27515-2288

BUSINESS REPLY MAIL
FIRST CLASS MAIL   PERMIT NO. 509   CHAPEL HILL, NC

Postage will be paid by addressee:

The University of North Carolina Press
Journals Fulfillment
Post Office Box 2288
Chapel Hill, NC 27515-2288

Table 1. Trends in Identification with the South* among Respondents Residing in the South, 1991–2001

	Estimated Decline from Trend Analysis	N in Sample
Overall (Since 1991)	−7.4%	17,186
Gender (since 1991)		
Female	−6.2%	9999
Male	−9.2%	7183
Race/Ethnicity (since 1991)		
Black	−4.4%	2781
White	−5.5%	12,550
Asian American, Native American (since 1992)	−9.5%	522
Hispanic only	−19.0%	959
Age (since 1991)		
17–34	−8.9%	5445
35–54	−6.4%	6998
55+	−8.9%	4646
Residence (since 1991)		
City/Suburban	−6.5%	8956
Town/Rural	−8.1%	8165
Appalachia	−6.3%	1211
Lowland	−7.0%	14,127
Deep South (AL, GA, LA, MS, SC)	−4.4%	5339
Peripheral South (AR, FL, KY, NC, OK, TN, TX, VA)	−8.3%	11,846
Years Lived in South (since 1992)		
Less than 10	−4.5%	1836
More than 10 but less than entire life	−5.3%	3717
Entire life	−2.1%	10,232
Education (since 1991)		
Less than high school	−5.5%	2035
High school	−9.6%	5155
Some college	−6.1%	4624
College and above	−3.9%	5290

Table 1. (continued)

	Estimated Decline from Trend Analysis	N in Sample
Marital Status (since 1991)		
Married	–4.0%	9044
Divorced, single, widowed	–8.6%	6959
Employment Status (since 1992)		
Employed	–6.5%	10,403
Unemployed/retired, etc.	–3.6%	4781
In school	–12.4%	837
Religion (since 1992)		
Baptist/Methodist	–1.7%	7811
Episcopal, Lutheran, Presbyterian	–1.5%	1450
Other protestant	–15.3%	2092
Catholic	–12.9%	2299
Other religion	–21.8%	1301
No religion	–1.5%	894
Income (since 1992)		
Less than 20K	–7.0%	3208
20–29.9K	–9.8%	2438
30–39.9K	–2.1%	2237
40–49.9K	–2.2%	1573
50–59.9K	–7.5%	1177
60K+	–0.8%	2765
Political Stance/Affiliation (since 1992)		
Conservative	–0.4%	5799
Moderate	–5.3%	4941
Liberal	–7.8%	3008
No preference	–18.9%	734
Democrat	–8.9%	5601
Republican	–0.1%	5183
Independent	–7.2%	3500

* Eleven former Confederate states plus Kentucky and Oklahoma.

Just about the time Hodding Carter III issued his highly visible salvo in *Time*, 82 percent of the 233 North Carolinians interviewed in the 1991 and 1992 Southern Focus Polls said they were southern. This is a bit higher than the percentage identifying with the region in the 1971 survey of the state. To the extent that North Carolinians broadly typify at least a segment of the upper or peripheral South, then, "southernness" as a self-declared identity had not declined at all, and possibly had risen, in the two decades of very real regional change since the Reed-Elder survey. What, though, of more recent, and more geographically dispersed, patterns? Has there been any detectable trend upward or downward since 1991 in the percentage of southerners who identify as "southerners?"

The Southern Focus Polls indicate that though considerable variability in southern identity exists from year to year, most residents of the region, 70 percent or more, continued throughout the 1990s and into the new century to identify as southern. (See figure 1. Keep in mind that for each of these figures the vertical axis represents the percentage of southern respondents, and the horizontal axis designates the year of the poll.) There is no question, then, of the extinction of self-declared southerners as a group, whatever the reality (or lack thereof) of vanishing southern distinctiveness. Moreover, to the extent that the existence of the South—at least as an imagined community—depends on the willingness of its residents to identify with the region, rather than their identity being a conse-

"Symbolic southerners" differentiate themselves from the mass of Americans by grounding their identity in a mythic place existing mainly in cultural memory. Photograph courtesy of Tennessee Tourist Development.

At the tail end of the Civil Rights era, the majority of southerners—roughly 80 percent—affirmed their southernness when told "Some people here think of themselves as Southern, others do not" and then asked, "How about you—would you say you are a Southerner or not?" Four African American student Civil Rights activists "sitting in" at the Woolworth lunch counter in Greensboro, North Carolina, courtesy of Greensboro News-Record Library.

quence of regional distinctiveness, as John Shelton Reed and others have argued, the region itself remains alive and well. That said, the poll data also indicate that identification as a southerner has clearly suffered a modest decline since 1991: according to the polls, southern identity has fallen, on average, about 0.7 of a percentage point per year since 1991, from a high percentage in the upper 70s eleven years ago to a (predicted) low hovering at 70 percent in 2001.[7]

Eleven years, admittedly, are not sufficient to establish an actual trend in regional identity. But there are several clues in the Focus Polls suggesting that the decrease since 1991 is not ephemeral. First is the near universality of the trend among southerners who are otherwise quite diverse: even those who, in the recent past, have been the most likely to identify as southern are now less likely to do so. Second is the static or, in some cases, declining traditional demographic base of "southernness" itself.

The decline in identification with the South is seen, usually fairly strongly, for both women and men (see figures 2 and 3) and for all races, ethnicities—especially Hispanics—(see figures 4, 5, and 6) and age groups (see figure 7, 8, and 9): Hispanic, black and white, male and female, young and old—all discernibly identify with the region less in 2001 than 1991. The decline is seen, too, for both urban and rural dwellers, for those living in the southern mountains and in the

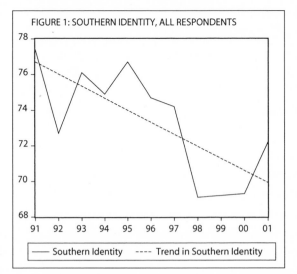

FIGURE 1: SOUTHERN IDENTITY, ALL RESPONDENTS

— Southern Identity   ---- Trend in Southern Identity

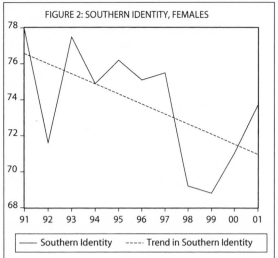

FIGURE 2: SOUTHERN IDENTITY, FEMALES

— Southern Identity   ---- Trend in Southern Identity

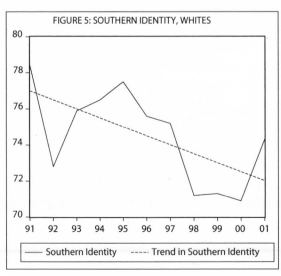

FIGURE 3: SOUTHERN IDENTITY, MALES

— Southern Identity   ---- Trend in Southern Identity

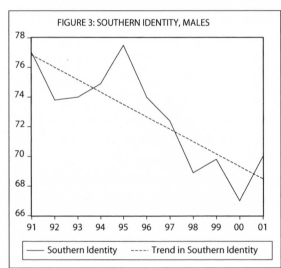

FIGURE 4: SOUTHERN IDENTITY, AFRICAN AMERICANS

— Southern Identity   ---- Trend in Southern Identity

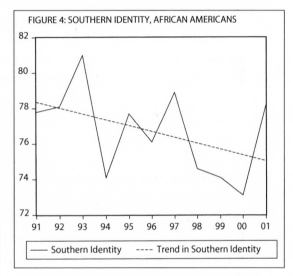

FIGURE 5: SOUTHERN IDENTITY, WHITES

— Southern Identity   ---- Trend in Southern Identity

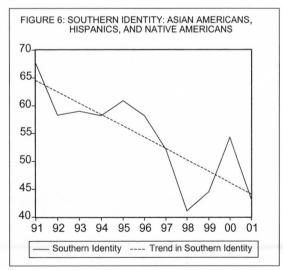

FIGURE 6: SOUTHERN IDENTITY: ASIAN AMERICANS, HISPANICS, AND NATIVE AMERICANS

— Southern Identity   ---- Trend in Southern Identity

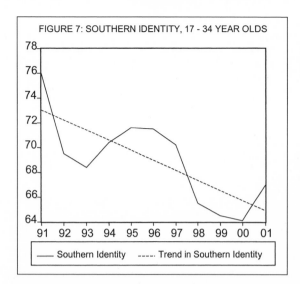

FIGURE 7: SOUTHERN IDENTITY, 17 - 34 YEAR OLDS

— Southern Identity   ----- Trend in Southern Identity

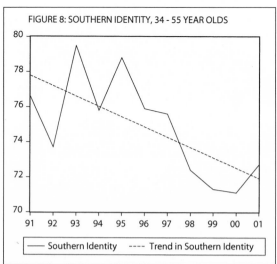

FIGURE 8: SOUTHERN IDENTITY, 34 - 55 YEAR OLDS

— Southern Identity   ---- Trend in Southern Identity

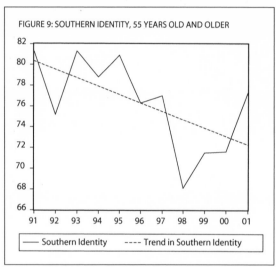

FIGURE 9: SOUTHERN IDENTITY, 55 YEARS OLD AND OLDER

— Southern Identity   ---- Trend in Southern Identity

lowlands, and for those in the deep as well as the peripheral South. It is observed for all education levels, all marital and employment groups, and most religious groups, income categories, and political affinities. Table 1 presents the estimated trend in regional identity for forty-six groups broken down by race, gender, age, education, and the like. The contraction of southern identity during the decade of the 1990s was minimal for mainline Protestants, obviously a huge group of southerners, and for the unchurched, but only the region's Republicans, political conservatives, and most affluent escaped the decline entirely. No category of geographic southerners among the forty-six groups increased their identification with the region during the period of the Southern Focus Poll. If variable across social groups in the region and not generally severe for most of them, the decline in southern identity nonetheless is quite pervasive.

The second reason that the downward movement in southern identity over the

last eleven years is not ephemeral is that the groups that have traditionally exhibited the highest degree of southernness are themselves somewhat less prevalent in the region's population as the convergence of region and nation continues. As a proportion of the South's population, lifelong southerners, rural southerners in the Deep South, and religious fundamentalists and Baptists (groups with a particular affinity for the South) are giving way, modestly but seemingly inexorably, to folks who are much less inclined to identify with the South. For example, three-fourths of Hispanics identified with the region in 1991–92; by 2000–01, only a bit more than half did. During this period, moreover, they increased their representation in the Southern Focus Polls by about 50 percent, from about 5 percent to more than 8 percent.[8] Likewise, southerners with religious identities other than mainline Protestant—those without traditional denominational anchoring and, to a lesser degree, Catholics—are proportionately more numerous in the region, up from approximately 33 percent in 1992–93 to more than 40 percent by the turn of the century. They are also shedding their southern identity at the rate of almost a percentage point a year: since 1992 the percentage identifying

The contraction of southern identity during the 1990s was minimal for mainline Protestants, obviously a huge group of southerners, and the unchurched. Only the region's Republicans, political conservatives, and most affluent escaped the decline entirely. Photograph courtesy of the Christian Broadcasting Network.

with the region has fallen from 65 to 58 percent. These and similar cultural shifts — and there are many — clearly do not augur well for the maintenance of southern identity at the high levels observed in the recent past.

Admittedly, these patterns should not be overstated. Too little over-time data exist here or elsewhere to gauge with certainty trends in regional identification. But with the Southern Focus Poll currently on hiatus, these eleven years of data may offer the only opportunity to study southern identity systematically over time with large numbers of randomly sampled, geographically diverse southerners.

These patterns also should not be projected without qualification into the future: what appears to be a trend today can be reversed tomorrow. As newcomers to the South, such as Hispanics, experience southern culture over a sustained period, for example, they may increasingly think of themselves as southern. By far the single strongest correlate of southern identity in these data, and one often overriding potentially competing racial, ethnic, and religious identities, is how long individuals have lived in the South. The downward trend for lifelong white southerners — most of whom do not have ready access to competing ethnic or racial identities, for example — was only about .5 percent during the eleven years of the poll. But what we see from the remaining poll data is not so encouraging. *All* lifelong southerners, black and white — more than 90 percent of whom have declared their southern identity in every poll — have reduced their identification rates by 2 percent since 1991. Among Hispanics who had lived in the region all their life, 81 percent identified as southern from 1991 to 1993, compared to less

Self-defined southerners are not a dying breed. They have not "vanished," and they have not been displaced by so-called cosmopolitans. But, proportionately, there are visibly fewer of them today than just a decade or so ago. Photograph courtesy of the Odum Photo Study in the Southern Historical Collection at The University of North Carolina at Chapel Hill.

than 74 percent in 1999 though 2001. The decline for lifelong southern Asian Americans, especially, and Native Americans was as precipitous: considered as a group, their rates of regional self-categorization fell from 88 percent in 1992–93 to 81 percent in 1999–2001.

It is not easy to imagine a circumstance that would dramatically reverse the patterns seen in these data. Pockets of the rural lowland and mountain South aside, the region is likely to continue to converge with nation: the South of tomorrow will be more urban, home to more newcomers, and display greater religious and ethnic diversity. Southern identity is apt to suffer as a consequence. In a post-"9/11" America, finally, regional identity of any sort—including identification with the South—may for an extended period take a backseat to a resurgence of national consciousness and identity. Self-defined southerners are not a dying breed; they have not "vanished," and they have not been displaced by so-called cosmopolitans. But, proportionately, there are visibly fewer of them today than just a decade or so ago for two reasons. First, southern identity's core constituencies have shrunk, and, second, for now at least, most groups of southerners—including some of those usually most closely identified with the South—have cooled somewhat in their enthusiasm for the label "southern." The region apparently no longer mobilizes the identities of its citizens as strongly as it did just a decade or so ago. Why exactly this has happened and whether this should be met with chagrin or relief are questions for future analysis.

Read More About It

Harry S. Ashmore, *An Epitaph for Dixie* (Norton, 1958).

John B. Boles, "The New Southern History," *Mississippi Quarterly* (Fall, 1992): 369–83.

Leslie W. Dunbar, "The Final New South?," *Virginia Quarterly Review* (Winter, 1998): 49–58.

John Egerton, *The Americanization of Dixie: the Southernization of America* (Harper's Magazine Press, 1974).

David Goldfield, *Still Fighting the Civil War: The American South and Southern History* (Louisiana State University Press, 2002).

Selz C. Mayo, "Social Change, Social Movements and Disappearing Sectional South," *Social Forces* (October, 1964): 1–10

John C. McKinney and Linda Brookover Bourque, "The Changing South: National Incorporation of a Region," *American Sociological Review* (June, 1971): 399–412.

Howard L. Preston, "Will Dixie Disappear? Cultural Contours of a Region in Transition," *The Future South* (University of Illinois Press, 1991), 188–216.

John Shelton Reed, "The Banner That Won't Stay Furled," *Southern Cultures* (Spring, 2002): 76–99.

———, "The South's Mid-Life Crisis," and "New South or No South? Southern Culture in 2036," in John Shelton Reed, *My Tears Spoiled My Aim and Other Reflections on Southern Culture* (Harcourt Brace, 1993).

———, James M. Kohls, and Carol Hanchette, "The Shrinking South and the Dissolution of Dixie," *Social Forces* (September, 1990): 221–33.

Leonard Reissman, "Social Development and the American South," *Journal of Social Issues* (January, 1966): 101–16.

Charles P. Roland, "The Ever-Vanishing South," *Journal of Southern History* (February, 1982): 3–20.

NOTES

We would like to thank Peggy Thoits and John Willis for their comments on this paper.

1. Hodding Carter III, "The End of the South," *Time*, 6 August 1990, 82.

2. James C. Cobb, "An Epitaph for the North: Reflections on the Politics of Regional and National identity at the Millennium," *Journal of Southern History* (February, 2000): 3–24; Larry J. Griffin, "Southern Distinctiveness, Yet Again: Or, Why America Still Needs the South," *Southern Cultures* 6 (Fall 2000): 51–76.

3. Benedict Anderson, *Imagined Communities* (Verso, 1991), 6–7. Our notion of "symbolic southernness" is heavily indebted to the sociologist Herbert J. Gans, who developed the intriguing notion of "symbolic ethnicity" to account for the upsurge of ethnic identity among largely assimilated second- and third-generation (nonsouthern) white ethnics. See Gans, "Symbolic Ethnicity: The Future of Ethnic Groups and Cultures in America," *Ethnic and Racial Studies* 2.1: 1–20.

4. John Shelton Reed, *Southerners: The Social Psychology of Sectionalism* (University of North Carolina Press, 1983), 12. The Southern Focus Poll was conducted by the UNC Odum Institute for Research in Social Science and sponsored by the Atlanta *Journal-Constitution* and the UNC Center for the Study of the American South. Polling data can be accessed online at http://www2.irss.unc.edu/irss/pollstories/sfpollindex.asp, 9 April 2003. The 1991 poll, also administered by UNC, appears to be a precursor to the Focus Polls.

5. The 1991 poll sampled southerners only and excluded Oklahoma; though not strictly comparable to the Focus Polls, its biases, especially when appropriately weighted, appear to be small.

6. See the distinction Reed (*Southerners*, 11, 56) draws between these two forms of identification. The Southern Focus Polls asked respondents about identification with other southerners too infrequently to permit assessment of trend. For analysis linking identification *as* a southerner with identification *with* others in the region in the polls, see Larry J. Griffin and Peggy A. Thoits, "Region as Social Identity: Do You Consider Yourself a Southerner?" (unpublished, 2003).

7. "From that point of view, the question is, in the first place, less geographical than social-psychological; it is less that southerners are people who come from the South, for instance, than that the South is where Southerners come from." John Shelton Reed, *One South: An Ethnic Approach to Regional Culture* (University of North Carolina Press, 1986), 13.

This trend line is derived from a statistical procedure called regression analysis. Procedures to detect trends which use all data points to calculate the extent of change, such as regression analysis, generate more reliable results than do simple comparisons of beginning and ending scores, which, given the entire history of the series, may be unusually high or low due merely to the idiosyncrasies of a particular sample (e.g., over-sampling of a particular group).

Separate trend analyses were conducted for each of the thirteen states surveyed in the Southern Focus Polls: only Arkansans increased their regional identification over the eleven years of the poll, and that gain was quite modest (about 2 percent). Trends for the remaining twelve states were all negative, with Texans and North Carolinians leading the psychological withdrawal from the region (11 to 12 percent decline). The trends in the table and graphs were calculated by using as the base only those respondents who answered the identity question "yes" or "no," but analysis including "don't know" responses and refusals produced nearly identical results.

8. See also the Associated Press release of 4 September 2002, "Census: South Sees Fastest U.S. Hispanic Population Growth." The AP story, based on a Census report, noted that since 1994 the Hispanic population has grown almost 24 percent in the (Census-defined) South, compared to 19 percent for the country as a whole. Hispanics in the region are concentrated in Florida and Texas, but Arkansas, Georgia, and North Carolina comprise three of the four states in the nation with the steepest Hispanic growth rates.

"Looking for Railroad Bill"
On the Trail of an Alabama Badman

by Burgin Mathews

ailroad Bill, the "notorious Negro desperado" of Escambia County, Alabama, stepped into Tidmore and Ward's general store in the small railroad community of Atmore on March 7, 1896; he left the store dead, his body riddled with bullets, his face and right hand mangled. "About fifteen pistol, rifle and gunshot wounds were found," the local *Pine Belt News* reported. "It was the opinion [of the examiner] that the first shot fired by [Constable] J. L. McGowan would have proved fatal." The fourteen or so others, however, ceremoniously and beyond any lingering doubt closed the case. The full story ran the next morning in newspapers across Alabama. "The forces were all concentrated around Atmore," Montgomery's *Daily Advertiser* announced, "for they knew that that small station was destined to be the theatre where the curtain would be rung down on the last act of Railroad Bill's bloody career. It was rung all right last night."[1]

Later that week, the *Pine Belt News* rendered the event in the same theatrical terms, proclaiming "the curtain was unceremoniously rung down on Saturday night." The language of the "theatre," the "last act," and the "curtain . . . rung down" created a dramatic finale long awaited by many of Alabama's citizens. For over a year, newspapers had indeed put on a show, a morality play steeped in melodrama and violence, and in a final, grisly climax the show had at last come to its anticipated end.[2]

Railroad Bill began his career around 1893 as a turpentine still worker named Morris Slater. According to the often repeated story, Slater had refused to pay any tax on his Winchester rifle and instead, in the words of the Montgomery *Advertiser*, "bid defiance to the world in general." A couple of policemen confronted Slater, ordering him to hand over the weapon or face arrest; Slater walked away, was shot at, and shot back. Deputy Sheriff Allen Brewton was wounded in the ear, and Slater escaped into the swamps or, according to some later accounts, onto a passing train. Over the next two years, Morris Slater—known forever after as "Railroad Bill"—terrorized trains, illegally riding the south Alabama freighters, often robbing them of their goods and occasionally engaging in shootouts with

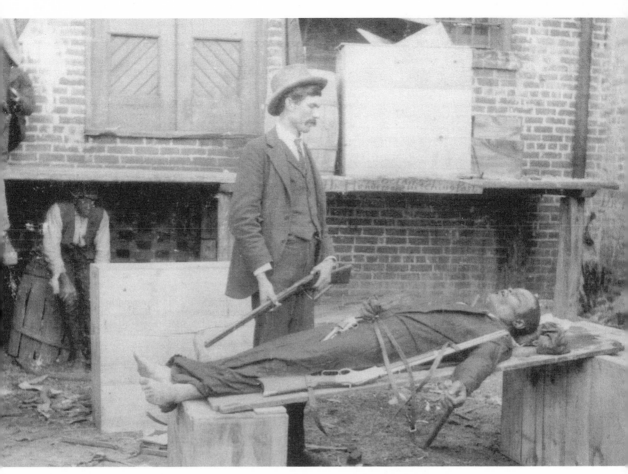

*The first bullet that Constable J. L. McGowan fired into Railroad Bill would probably have been enough—
but over a dozen more shots made sure the outlaw was really dead. J. L. McGowan standing over the body of
Railroad Bill, courtesy of the Estate of Ed Leigh McMillan Trust.*

resisting trainmen or police. Eventually, in one of those shootouts, he added murder to his record, and by 1895 he was the most wanted criminal in the state. And,
most significant to his unfolding legend, he was black.[3]

Alabama had recently emerged from Reconstruction and with the rest of the
South struggled to adjust to a new racial as well as economic order. During the
1890s white southerners fought to contain black autonomy, creating codes of
segregation and developing the corresponding codes of racial violence; lynching
had become a regional pastime, enacted publicly and with unprecedented regularity. In an effort to assert their supremacy, whites constructed a unified racial
identity and responded with fear and violence to an emancipated and, they
thought, unruly African American population. Within this context, the legend of
Railroad Bill became a stage on which the white South enacted its bloody drama
of race, identity, and power. For white southerners, the elusive character justified
their fear of black autonomy as well as the need for retaliation. The hunt for Rail-

road Bill, which reached its greatest intensity between the summer of 1895 and the following March, pitted the black demon against the vast and righteous arm of a loosely configured body of white law enforcement; the curtain rung down in Atmore signified plainly the end of Railroad Bill's reign of terror. The white fear of black autonomy, however, would remain, enhanced by the events of the preceding months. And while the law and the press—the white South's most visible extensions—had created from the real life of Morris Slater an allegory of good and evil, black southerners reacted—and, to some degree, retaliated—with their own, also powerful, visions of the outlaw.

THE COLOR OF THE OUTLAW

Railroad Bill's character reached mythic proportions during his own lifetime, and his legend was destined only to grow in death. Color was essential to Bill's identity, and in twentieth-century memory, his very blackness grew to a legendary scale. In 1931 the *Atmore Advance* remembered Bill as a "stout and coal-black man." A 1971 *History of Baldwin County* depicted him as "a big dark-brown Negro," and Marjorie Jagendorf's *Folk Stories of the South*, published the following year, proclaimed in colorful, sentimental prose: "Bill was black as ebony and strong as Samson of the Bible."[4]

If a coal-and-ebony or dark-brown blackness, always complemented by a corresponding "bigness," was the preferred image of Bill in these twentieth-century retellings, contemporary reports had to make do with Bill's actual, lighter skin. Newspapers identified their villain as a "yellow negro," his tone a "gingerbread color." A proclamation posted for his capture in April 1895 described the out-

While the Alabama outlaw lived, his escapades provided fodder for gossip, rumor, and countless newspaper stories across the region. After his death, stories about him endured in white and African American folklore alike. Cartoons of Railroad Bill's exploits from L & N Employees' *Magazine, May 1927.*

law's "face [as] dark yellow as if sunburned or smoked," his "breast and stomach to the waist light yellow." Despite the obstacles of this relative lightness, however, newspapers emphasized Railroad Bill's blackness as much as possible, racializing the villain beyond the limits of his "yellow" skin. Reports referred redundantly to Bill as a "black Negro," doubling if not his physical blackness, then his cultural, biological, or psychological blackness. In one article he was a "black scoundrel" who "thirsted for blood," his color merging with an almost inhuman evil. In other articles he appeared repeatedly as "the dusky desperado" or "the dusky demon," his "deeds of darkness" suggesting not only deeds of evil, but also deeds characteristic of a dark people.

The dehumanizing and often inflammatory rhetoric of the newspaper descriptions served to fuel white animosity toward both Bill and the race that he embodied; as the lawless career of Railroad Bill demonstrated, all black men were potentially scoundrels and demons if they slipped from the control of white authority. Railroad Bill's "deeds of darkness" did indeed carry a double and urgent meaning when even a yellow or gingerbread blackness and its inherent evil reigned unchecked in a land of supposed white supremacy. Within representations of the outlaw, then, Bill was fundamentally black, and his blackness gave the story its central symbol and its emotional power. Newspapers made frequent use of the derogatory names of the day, referring derisively to Bill and his companions as "darkies." "One thing is for certain," the *Pine Belt News* reported in August of 1895 in the clear manner of a call to arms, "Bill is still a free nigger and wanders at his will."[5]

THE DEATH OF MCMILLAN

In his analysis of the development of the black folk hero, folklorist John W. Roberts argues that with the abolition of slavery the legal systems of the South replaced the slave system as the framework through which southern whites maintained control over blacks. Legal segregation, vagrancy laws, and voting restrictions, with the convict lease system and chain gang labor instituted as means of criminal punishment, bounded tightly the limits of black freedom. Largely in response to the injustices of the law, the prototype of the badman emerged as the dominant hero of African American folklore at the turn of the century. And, as sociologist H. C. Brearley has noted, the shift in the institutional control of black life by white society brought about the policeman as the ultimate embodiment of white authority—and, in turn, the ultimate object of the badman's violent opposition.[6]

Such symbolism was entrenched by the 1890s not only in the folklore of black southerners, but in all arenas of southern society, reflected in the very fabric of the white legal system and the press. On the evening of July 3, 1895, Railroad Bill

When news of Sheriff E. S. McMillan's death reached his hometown of Brewton, residents cancelled the Fourth of July festivities that they had been planning for months. McMillan, courtesy of the Estate of Ed Leigh McMillan Trust.

shot and killed Sheriff E. S. McMillan of Brewton, Alabama, who had tracked him to a Florida swamp a few miles south of the state border. "Recently," the Montgomery *Advertiser* reported, "Sheriff McMillan organized a posse and started out to nab the darkie." The *Pine Belt News* continued the story: "They traced him to Bluff Springs [Florida] and by means of a Negro man (and there came the trouble) they located him at a house about a half mile above the station." In the shootout that ensued, McMillan was fatally wounded, and Bill, believed to be hit in the return volley, escaped. A special train brought the sheriff's wife and friends from Brewton, but McMillan was dead by the time the train arrived.[7]

Sheriff McMillan's death was a source of shock, sadness, and terror to the county's white citizens; the sheriff's noble reputation seems to have been as well known as Bill's own, opposite reputation, and the tragedy made real the worst fears of the community. News of the sheriff's death reached Brewton on the morning of the fourth of July, and the town canceled the holiday festivities, which had been months in the planning. When the day arrived, the Montgomery *Adver-*

tiser announced "Universal Sorrow at the Death of a Good Man and Brave Officer" and "deep gloom over the little town" of Brewton. "A feeling of sadness pervades this entire county," the paper mourned. "Rain has been falling nearly all day, creeks and rivers are swollen to overflowing and it still rains." Railroad Bill had effectively destroyed the plans and hopes for the white holiday—in June the paper had predicted "a barbecue, blow-out, etc." to "eclipse all attempts of the past"—and the simple coincidence of timing reinforced fears of Bill and other black men like him as literal threats to white independence, freedom, and security. "Last Thursday, July 4th, will go down in history as one of the gloomiest days that was ever spent by Brewtonites," the *Pine Belt News* predicted, solemnly registering the shift in spirit from holiday elation to communal mourning:

> The deplorable news of the tragic death of a citizen loved by all and for whom every one had the highest regard caused our people to abandon all ideas of celebrating the national holiday. Instead of the usual rejoicing incident to this day there would be mourning. Our town instead of being in holiday attire would be appropriately decked in crepe, out of respect to Sheriff McMillan, who had been ruthlessly murdered at Bluff Springs the previous night.[8]

Newspapers made as much of McMillan's heroism and the tragedy of his death as they did of Bill's villainy, inspiring sympathy in their characterization of the survivors—including an "aged mother" and the "devoted wife"—and emphasizing the sheriff's compassion as well as his bravery and devotion to duty. "He was a fearless official," the *Advertiser* eulogized, "who went about the duties of his office and discharged them in such a way as to win the confidence and esteem of all with whom he came into contact. He was considered a terror to evil-doers—very few criminals ever evaded him a long time. A good man, a true husband, affectionate son and brother, has thus passed away!" The paper also named McMillan "one of the bravest and best men in Alabama, and one of the very few whom 'Railroad' feared." And although the train that brought McMillan's wife to the scene of the shootout reached the sheriff after he had died, at least one report increased the sentimental and sympathetic power of the final scene by adding a few minutes to the sheriff's life: "When the special train arrived at Bluff Springs," the *Advertiser* reported, "the brave officer was in the throes of death, expiring a few minutes afterwards in the arms of his wife." The press's representation of McMillan thus personalized the law, personifying it in the form of the sheriff who was also husband, father, and friend. In the days to follow, the public sorrow and sympathy inspired by the event and reinforced by its sentimental retellings translated swiftly into fear of and rage toward the killer.[9]

With the death of McMillan, the hunt for Railroad Bill took a critical turn in its meaning and scale. If the policeman was the living embodiment of white authority, then his death at the hands of the black desperado symbolized the direct con-

The Alabama outlaw was a particular menace to local railroads, illegally riding the cars and robbing freighters of their goods. Small wonder that the L&N Railroad contributed both its detectives and $350 worth of reward money to the hunt for Railroad Bill. Montgomery Railyard (below) and the L&N Railroad Office at Montgomery in 1887 (above), courtesy of the Alabama Department of Archives and History.

frontation and temporary overthrowing of that power. Such symbolism appealed to many African Americans, who fashioned terrible but powerful heroes out of criminals whose actions they could not approve of but nonetheless had to admire as alternatives to the silent complacency assigned African Americans in southern society. The meaning of the event was equally evident to whites, to whom it represented the confirmation of deep-rooted prejudices and fears, and they committed themselves to doing all in their power to reclaim their supremacy while avenging the death of their own hero. The moment of McMillan's murder consequently became the focal point of both black and white recreations of Bill's career. Indeed, it was the turning point in the development of the chase, launching the outlaw and his pursuers into the dramatic second act of their shared career.

"Thursday afternoon," the *Pine Belt News* reported, "about two dozen well-armed and indignant citizens left for the scene of the killing for the avowed purpose of avenging the killing of our highly esteemed and brave officer of the law." Over the next several months, the hunt for Railroad Bill escalated dramatically. The L&N Railroad Company offered a $350 reward for Bill's capture, along with a lifetime railroad pass. The state of Alabama added $150 to the reward, the state of Florida $200, the citizens of Brewton $300, and the citizens of Escambia County $250, for a total reward of $1,250. "From now on," Montgomery's *Advertiser* predicted, "the trail promises to be exceedingly warm. That $1,250 reward will attract the slickest 'sleuth-hounds' in the country."[10]

That reward, coupled for many white males with a sense of social and racial obligation, did indeed put an extensive cast of characters on Railroad Bill's trail. At its peak, the manhunt incorporated officers of the law and "indignant citizens" from several Alabama and Florida counties, packs of dogs from the state penitentiary, L&N Railroad detectives, Pinkerton agents, at least two undercover black detectives, and a number of self-employed bounty hunters from places as distant as Texas and Indiana. "At present," the *Advertiser* reported on July 10, 1895, "there are some twenty-five pursuers of the badly wanted scoundrel." The following day, the same paper noted, "There are now more than fifty men on the hunt for the criminal, so it is said, and surely they shall have no trouble in catching him sooner or later." By August 2 the number had become a "small army," the paper counting "at least one hundred men here loaded for bear." Two days later, a reporter editorialized that the numbers had in fact grown *too* large to be effective: "There are entirely too many men after him to ever effect his capture," the newsman wrote. "A dozen men and the blood hounds now here would soon run to earth the daring rascal if Tom, Dick and Harry and nearly everybody else did not have a gun, rifles, or musket on their shoulder, some wishing they would never see Bill alive."[11]

If in the symbolic terms of Railroad Bill's career the law was synonymous with white authority, it was the tacit duty of all whites—down to the bungling Tom, Dick, and Harry—to protect that authority. The law by definition was white and male; blackness, in turn, became the shade of the outlaw. The hunt for Railroad Bill, then, emerged in popular culture as a battle enacted within the strict terms of racial categories. Shortly after the death of McMillan, the Escambia County town of Alco reported that "four of Alco's pale faces returned from Bluff Springs Saturday afternoon where they had been hunting 'Railroad Bill.'" The conception of the hunt in terms of paleness versus darkness, evoking here a game of cowboys and Indians, suggested the myth of an immutable color bar, rigidly segregating black and white into the roles peculiar to their skin colors—notably that of the

Many white commentators portrayed the hunt for Railroad Bill within a framework that was especially powerful in turn-of-the-century America: white hunters versus the dark-skinned hunted, paleness disciplining darkness, white western heroes administering frontier justice to Indians. Illustration from Wild Life on the Plains and the Horrors of Indian Warfare, *published by Royal Publishing Co. in 1891.*

white male dutifully administering justice to the black male, the latter envisioned as the famous and faceless "bad nigger." Thus the figure of Railroad Bill, while representing a powerful individual threat to white authority, conveniently provided a means of dramatizing and solidifying the racial dualities upon which Alabama and the South had come to rely since Reconstruction and the recent birth of segregation.[12]

Throughout the summer of 1895, many African Americans in and beyond south Alabama paid heavily for Railroad Bill's individual "deeds of darkness." On July 5 the Montgomery *Advertiser* reported, under the headline "Several Negroes in Jail at Pensacola and One Held at Bluff Springs," that a "deputy sheriff came in on the 7 o'clock train tonight with Peter Roebuck, Albert Williams, Henry Washington, Sallie Rankins, Mary Johnson, Lizzie Payne, and Mollie Jackson, all Negroes, charged with harboring and protecting Bill. They were all lodged in the county jail." The black man who had acted as a scout for McMillan before his death and who many citizens believed knowingly led their sheriff into a trap was being "held by the citizens of Bluff Springs." Later that week, another group of African Americans found themselves subject to violence at the hands of the army-sized posse: "It has been learned from a reliable source," the *Advertiser* reported, "that the posse that went out in pursuit of him found quite a number of Negroes who had been harboring the Negro desperado, and that they took them out in the woods and whipped them soundly, with the admonition that they might expect something more severe if they persisted in their conduct." Here, in a rare instance of the press's sympathy for the African Americans involved, the reporter noted the predicament of innocent people caught in a racially defined war: "These Negroes," the report continued,

> may now be said to be between the "devil and the deep blue sea," for if they do not give "Railroad" whatever he demands of them he is more than liable to perforate their anatomies with sundry pellets of lead; and if they do so and the white folks find it out they will no doubt inflict summary punishment. The question arises, would it not be better for these Negroes to leave that section of the country?[13]

Leaving, of course, was an impractical solution, and African Americans found their situations only worsening as the law honed in on Bill. In late July Railroad Bill disappeared into Murder Creek Swamp, near the Conecuh County town of Castleberry, and white forces penetrated the swamp in search of their game. A Montgomerian who had visited that region in order to join the hunt described the roles performed by both blacks and whites in relation to the criminal: "All the negroes in that neighborhood are harboring and helping him all they can," he told a reporter. "The entire country is aroused, and every [white] man in the neighborhood is out with his gun on a dead hunt for William." Descriptions of the swamp itself reflected racist assumptions, as the Montgomery paper repeatedly referred to the south Alabama region as a "jungle," evoking images of Africa, wild beasts and primitive people. L&N Detective T. J. Watts characterized the swamp in purely legendary terms, indulging in rhetoric both mythical and racist in its implications. "It is simply the wildest country you ever saw," he informed a reporter:

> Why there are thirty foot alligators with moss on their backs, bears and all sorts of game and wild beasts. "Railroad" knows the lay of the land so well that I shouldn't doubt but that he is "in" with the bears. It is certain that all the darkies will protect him if the bears won't.

Such a "certainty" translated ultimately into grounds for legal, and vigilante, action. The white assumption of a single black consciousness, expressed in both the above accounts, criminalized all African Americans through their supposed association with Bill, forcing anyone with black skin into the role of the outlaw; the "suspicious" or "suspicious looking Negro" became a common trope in the language of the press, and African Americans faced an increasing frequency of arrests and abuse. "A number of Negroes have been arrested," wired an operator from Castleberry on August 1. "None of them will be permitted to go about for fear that they might sneak some information to Railroad." "We are guarding all trains and arresting all Negroes who come along," Sheriff Irwin of Conecuh County declared that day, and on August 4 a special telegram from Brewton announced that "several suspicious negroes have been arrested within the past few days. Two or three boys have been released, and one or two are in jail. Some seem to think they are pals of Railroad."[14]

Others, still less fortunate, were mistaken for Bill himself. Five days after the death of McMillan, a telegram from Evergreen, Alabama, reported that "Sheriff R. F. Irwin, of this [Conecuh] county, arrested a suspicious looking negro here today, answering very well to the description of 'Railroad Bill.'" A corre-

White Alabamans' fears of Railroad Bill meant that many African American men were considered likely accomplices because of the color of their skin. An August 1895 telegram from Brewton reported that "several suspicious Negroes have been arrested within the past few days. . . . Some seem to think they are pals of Railroad." The courthouse at Brewton, Alabama, courtesy of the Alabama Department of Archives and History.

spondent for the Montgomery *Advertiser* interviewed the suspect, who confessed, "This is not the first time I have been arrested for Railroad Bill." The interview continued,

> "If you prove to be 'Railroad' you will have a tough time," your correspondent said to him.
> "I'm afraid I'll have a tough time anyhow."
> "Why?" asked the newspaper man.
> "Because they say I look just like him," he answered after some hesitation.

The following day, the man, identified as other than Railroad Bill, was released, "at once 'hit the grit,' and began 'counting crossties' in the direction of Atlanta as fast as his nether limbs could carry him."[15]

A few days later, a headline in the *Pine Belt News* announced: "THE WRONG MAN SHOT." "Near Pensacola last Friday," the article elaborated, "Bill Vaughan shot another negro whom he supposed to be Railroad." Again, a correspondent interviewed the wounded man: "He talked freely, saying that his name is Ed. Walden and that he had been working near Repton, Ala. He denies having a pistol or rifle and claims that Vaughan had no cause to shoot him. It is probable that he will recover." No subsequent article either confirmed or denied Walden's recovery. In weeks to come, however, newspapers noted similar incidents occurring far beyond the reaches of Railroad Bill's terrain. On August 13 the Montgomery *Advertiser* announced, "Sheriff P. B. Dorian has received a letter from a friend of his at Houston, Texas, stating that there is now in jail at that place a negro who answers the description of the much wanted and much hunted 'Railroad Bill,' and says that he has secured the promise of the sheriff at Houston to hold the suspicious negro till he hears from Sheriff Dorian."[16]

Four days after the report of this "Texas Railroad Bill," a Georgia train brought the "Corpse of a Negro who may be Railroad Bill" into Montgomery. According to the article, whose headline asked hopefully, "Is this the Wanted William?" an argument between two white Georgians and two "suspicious looking negroes" near Chipley, Georgia, resulted in the death of one of the black men. A man named Willis Garner had fired the fatal shot and had himself suffered from a less serious wound; his father arrived at the scene in time to examine and question the "wounded darkie." "The first thing we did was to go through his pockets," the elder Garner told the *Advertiser*.

> In them we found the circular (the one describing Railroad Bill and offering a reward for him), one or two packs of cards and a ticket for Pensacola. . . . I then asked him how he came to have the description of Railroad Bill in his pocket, and he became confused asking what description and trying to get out of having it. He was shot at 9 o'clock in the morning and died at 5 o'clock in

Like boxer Jack Johnson, Railroad Bill entered African American folklore as a character in the "bad nigger" tradition. Photographs of the championship fighter from Jack Johnson—In the Ring and Out, *by Jack Johnson, published by the National Sports Publishing Company in 1927.*

the afternoon, and during the whole day the only thing he would say when I asked him if he was Railroad Bill was "maybe I am, and maybe I ain't."

Sightings of Bill had lately come into the paper, the article continued, but the identities of the suspects, living and dead, remained undetermined. Six months later, after the death of the man ultimately declared to be Bill, the *Advertiser* further observed, "The number of negroes who were killed under the impression that they were Slater will never be known. Several were shot in Florida, Georgia, Mississippi and even out in Texas, but only one was brought here to be identified."[17]

RAILROAD BILL AND THE ORAL TRADITION

While the hunt for Railroad Bill escalated into a widening chain of racial violence—and as the press daily expanded upon the bloody record of the villain—Bill's exploits also entered a rich oral tradition among black southerners. Just as the printed press shaped its own image of Bill, black folklore embraced and recreated the character according to its own traditional conventions. Like the mythic gambler Stackolee before him and popular boxer Jack Johnson after him, the character of Railroad Bill fit neatly into the tradition of the black badman, the so-called "bad nigger" who defied white society at all costs. The badmen of black culture were the robbers, murderers, and gamblers who embodied a self-empowering, if ultimately self-destructive, force in the midst of an oppressive and debasing culture. Part trickster, part conjurer, and part outlaw, the badman resembled what historian Eric Hobsbawm, in his social analysis of banditry, has labeled the "avenger." These figures, according to Hobsbawm, achieve their heroic stature through the exertion not of justice but of terror, demonstrating the possibilities of power and violence within the lives of a weak or victimized people. While the majority of black men and women may not have condoned the actions of a Railroad Bill and likely even feared him, they could nonetheless admire and respect his power. Though Railroad Bill's deadly reputation surely frightened blacks and whites alike, Bill's embodiment of power made him a natural subject for the heroic myths of black culture.[18]

Tales sprang up that fashioned Railroad Bill as a conjurer who could only be killed by a silver bullet, who could hoodoo the dogs off of his trail, and who could change his form into that of an animal—a sheep, hawk, or hound—to effect his escape. "The wonderful darkey is like the Phoenix," the *Advertiser* reported on August 7 under the improbable headline, "THE WONDERFUL NEGRO POPULARLY SUPPOSED TO BE SUPERHUMAN"; "he cannot be downed and rises from the ashes with all imaginable sang froid."

Some of the most preposterous stories are told by the negroes in that neighborhood—and though it seems incredible, some white people who should know better, not only repeat these remarkable bogey tales with great gusto, but actually believe them. This class of people are firmly convinced that Railroad Bill has the superhuman power of easily transforming himself into any object, animate or inanimate, that he wants to.[19]

In his novel *Train Whistle Guitar*, black author Albert Murray (who was born in Bill's Escambia County in 1916) captures the persona celebrated by many south Alabama African Americans in their hero. "He was the one," Murray writes, "that no jail could hold overnight and no bloodhounds could track beyond a certain point."

> Because he worked a mojo on them that nobody had ever heard of before or since. And the last time he broke jail, they had the best bloodhounds in the whole state there to track him. But the next morning they found them all tied together in a fence corner near the edge of the swamp, not even barking anymore, just whining, and when they got them untangled they were ruined forever, couldn't scent a polecat and wouldn't even run a rabbit; and nobody saw or came near hide nor hair of Railroad Bill from that time on.[20]

Though historians, local-color writers, and the odd novelist have documented the narrative legends surrounding Bill, the many songs about the legend provide the fullest and most accurate sources for folk conceptions of Railroad Bill. These songs passed through oral tradition throughout the South, eventually entering the repertoires of white as well as black singers. Numerous verses of "Railroad Bill" were collected throughout the twentieth century and printed in collections by Howard Odum, John and Alan Lomax, Carl Sandburg and others; a few commercial recordings of "Railroad Bill" were released in the twenties and thirties, largely by white "hillbilly" musicians, and folklorists continued to document variants of the song as late as the 1980s. Though the texts and tunes vary, Railroad Bill songs follow the common structure identified by folklorist D. K. Wilgus as the "blues ballad." Unlike other ballads, this song-type provides no linear narrative but simply refers to the events of a story, presumably known to the community in which the song is traditionally performed. Dispensing with chronology and exact detail, the blues ballad celebrates rather than narrates events, improvising on the themes of the shared story. As the song moves in time and place from the original events, the details become still more diffuse, often leaving the personality or lifestyle of the hero as the sole focus of the verses; thus, in the Railroad Bill songs, it is most often not Bill's historical actions but the persona of the badman that is remembered and celebrated..[21]

One narrative event that does appear with considerable regularity in different renderings of "Railroad Bill," though, is the shooting of McMillan. "Railroad Bill made a mighty dash," a frequently collected verse states; "Shot McMillan by a

Songs about the legend of Railroad Bill became popular with both African American and white singers. Some of these verses were collected and printed by folklorists such as Howard Odum (left) and Alan Lomax (right). Photographs courtesy of the Southern Historical Collection at University of North Carolina at Chapel Hill and the collections of the Library of Congress respectively.

lightening flash / Talking 'bout that Negro, Railroad Bill." The arrests, beatings, and murders to which many African Americans found themselves subject between July 1895 and March 1896 also found their way into the badman folklore. One ballad verse pictures its singer unjustly mistaken for Railroad Bill—

> Standin' on the corner didn't mean no harm
> Policeman grab me by the arm,
> Wus lookin' fer Railroad Bill.

—while another explicitly condemns the martyred white hero whose name personified the racist law:

> McMillan kept riding all around,
> Handcuffing Negroes and carrying them down.
> All 'bout that Negro, Railroad Bill.

Here McMillan seems to deserve what he ultimately gets. In a similar verse, the singer is even more overt in his distaste for the sheriff and his resulting identification with Bill:

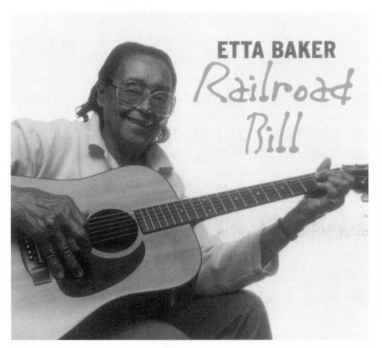

> Ed McMillan was the boss of the town
> Handcuffing negroes and hauling them around.
> I'm going to be like Railroad Bill.

Though most singers offered more ambiguous allegiance, fearing or disapproving of Bill's cruelty while applauding his strength, the rare assertion that "I'm going to be like Railroad Bill" recognizes violence as the only means of combating a degraded social position. Inspired by the facelessness of his situation, the singer strives to emulate, at least in song, the actions of the badman, ironically embracing the identity automatically assigned him by the law. While singers often confessed in their songs, "I'm scared of Railroad Bill," or complained that "Railroad Bill, got so bad / Took all the money that the po' farmers had," many nonetheless found a vicarious thrill in their narratives of the outlaw's deeds, often appropriating his guns, lifestyle, or voice through their performance. Will Bennet, a black guitarist who recorded a version of "Railroad Bill" in 1929, may have found a temporary empowerment as he assumed the role of the badman:

> Buy me a gun just as long as my arm,
> Kill everybody ever done me wrong,
> Now I'm gonna ride, my Railroad Bill.[22]

In the drama of the white law and the black outlaw African Americans reacted with some ambivalence to their outlaw status. Such a status, though degrading and ultimately destructive, offered those who accepted it a means of rebellion, no matter how limited. Most often, the rebellion would be subtle or vicarious, enacted through the oral celebration of the badman. The singer's proclamation, "I'm gonna be like Railroad Bill," or, more typical in its ambiguity, the dying Chipley man's response, "Maybe I am, and maybe I ain't," reflects efforts to internalize the rebellious tactics of the "bad nigger" to effect his own survival and demand his own agency.

THE DEATH OF MORRIS SLATER

When, on March 7, 1896, the curtain was finally rung down in that Atmore store, the brother of the late Sheriff McMillan wired the news to railroad superintendent J. J. McKinney: "I have just received a message from McGowan that he had shot him," the wire ran. "Come down and rejoice with us." Constable Leonard McGowan had shot Railroad Bill; once hit, the *Pine Belt News* reported, Bill "dropped to the floor like a beef, and as he did so the firing became general, pistol balls flying fast and thick into the corpse." Beyond that, the details of the death were, predictably, blurred by contradictory accounts. Whether Bill walked into a trap or entered the store to the surprise of his hunters; whether he was uncharacteristically unarmed or went down shooting; whether he didn't make it past the threshold of the store or was, as the most popular version of the story has it, sitting on a barrel eating "crackers and cheese" when the bullets hit—all of these details are rendered unknowable by the inconsistency of the reports.[23]

Though newspaper and oral accounts blur the details of Bill's death with typical contradiction, the essence of the moment as it appeared in the white press was that the spirit of celebration postponed since the previous Fourth of July could finally take place. "Everyone," the *Pine Belt News* announced, "is rejoicing with the McMillan brothers." Thirty years later L&N detective J. B. Harlan, one of the many men who had been assigned the case, recalled the celebratory atmosphere that pervaded Brewton:

During the day the negroes, as well as the white people from all over that section came to view the remains. I would conservatively estimate the crowd at 3,000 people. It looked like a big crowd on circus day. The negroes came from all directions in ox carts, on mule-back, walked, and in every other way they could come through the pine woods to view the remains of the noted negro desperado who had been killed. One negro woman made a great speech, warning all the other negroes to not follow the steps that "Railroad Bill" had followed because it had shown conclusively that a life of that kind would come to a bad end and that the ordinary lead bullet would kill a negro desperado as easily as a silver bullet.

Upon arrival in Montgomery, Railroad Bill's body was met by "a perfect mob of curious people." Over the next few days, the public could pay a quarter to view the body on display in an empty train car. Turn-of-the-century downtown Montgomery, courtesy of the Alabama Department of Archives and History.

Thus the white narrative of Railroad Bill concluded with a spirit of celebration, coupled with the moralizing tone that made an ugly example of black lawlessness and violence. Symbolically, the drama closed with the restoration of the body to its white pursuers. When Bill's body arrived in Brewton by train, it was greeted by sizable crowds, "standing room being at a premium." After the celebration in that town, officials moved the corpse to Montgomery, where it again met "a perfect mob of curious people," but, the *Advertiser* reported, "scant gratification was given their curiosity, for the crowd became so enormous that the top had to be replaced on the coffin, which was put in the baggage room and admittance denied." For the next four days, however, admission was granted for twenty-five cents, the body "placed on exhibition in an empty freight car." Following their appearance in Montgomery, the mutilated remains of Railroad Bill, one hand mangled and face ripped open, toured train stations along the L&N throughout south Alabama and into Florida, where the corpse eventually disappeared into an unmarked grave. In Brewton, souvenir hunters could pay fifty cents for "Photographs of the Dead Bandit." In the picture, the lifeless form of Railroad Bill lies bound to a plank, his rifle strapped to his side and one of his pistols placed—suggestive of another, underlying aspect of the black menace—at his crotch. Above the body stood the triumphant figure of Constable McGowan, his own rifle resting in his hands, functioning symbolically both as a comfort to whites and as an unmistakable warning to blacks.[24]

The question of the body's ownership, answered emphatically by the white exhibitions and the sheriff's pose, was crucial to the narrative of Bill's life and death. During the 1890s, black bodies were marketable goods; under lynch rule, whites tortured, burned, and mutilated the bodies of black men, often dispensing their fingers and other parts as keepsakes. Within this tradition, the black outlaw was defined in strictly physical terms of blackness; in death, the black body must remain under the control of its white captors, or the moral of the story would be lost. By the time McGowan brought the outlaw's career to an end, Railroad Bill's body had come to be infused with meaning for whites and blacks alike. This highly contested body had become the primary grounds on which Railroad Bill and white society had negotiated power, the whites projecting onto the form, ironically identified by the press as a "worthless carcass," figures up to $1,250. The nebulous identities of Railroad Bill, identified as "Morris Slater, alias C. S. Slater, alias Railroad, alias Zeb, alias Colonel Slater, of Baldwin County," and sighted weekly all over the Deep South, multiplied: whites projected the identity onto a number of African Americans, while a few black men themselves assumed the role of Railroad Bill, and others—whites as well as blacks—fashioned tales long after Bill's death of the body's supernatural transformation.[25]

"The entire country around Perdido was at once aroused," the *Advertiser* reported at the first news of Railroad Bill's death, "and bold threats were made by the immense mob of negroes gathered there that they would take the body from the McGowan party." With the aid of reinforcements and an emergency switch engine, McGowan was able to keep the corpse from the mob and deliver it safely into the hands of the white authorities, who in turn flaunted it throughout the state. A local legend claimed that while the body was in Brewton, the young son of the deceased Sheriff McMillan placed a handful of bitterweed in its mouth, vengefully and conclusively asserting his own power over the lifeless form. An alternate legend, endowing the body with an agency beyond death, suggested that one of the men attending Bill's corpse was scratched and died of blood poisoning. In the days following Bill's death and exhibition, the *Pine Belt News* reported, "many cut buttons off his clothes, scraps of cloth, cartridges, etc. as souvenirs." And there were others who insisted that the body was not Bill's at all, that he had never died, and indeed, that he never would.[26]

In many ways, the story of Railroad Bill escaped the narrow, racially limited framework insisted upon by the law and the press. As the *Advertiser* noted, "some whites who should know better," actually believed with blacks the myths of Bill's transformations. That paper's recognition of a "class of people" who participated in such tales may have revealed more than it intended—that class as much as race defined Bill's identity and popular reactions to that identity. During the twentieth century, Railroad Bill ballads figured into the repertoires of white and black rural performers alike; indeed, it was a white "hillbilly" performer, Riley Puckett of the Skillet Lickers, who first recorded "Railroad Bill" in 1924, and white country acts dominated commercial recordings of the song throughout that decade. Various commentators have noted that during the decade following the Civil War, the

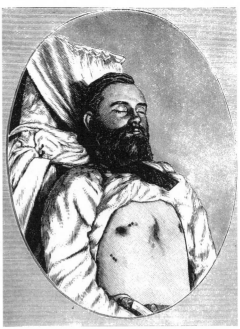

After the Civil War, widespread hostility to the railroad industry contributed to the popularity of
Railroad Bill and such other notorious outlaws as Jesse James, who, like Railroad Bill, met a bloody end.
James, from Illustrated Lives and Adventures of Frank and Jesse James *by Hon. J. A. Dacus,*
published by N. D. Thompson & Co. in 1882.

railroad—associated in the minds of many with wealthy businessmen, financial scandals, and economic exploitation—became a target of widespread public hostility; in this climate, figures such as Jesse James and Alabama's white outlaw Rube Burrow gained popularity for their opposition to railroads. It is possible that many rural, lower-class whites may have celebrated Bill's exploits alongside those of these other figures.[27]

The white, middle-class subjectivity of the press and the law, however, favored racial solidarity over class division, and happily translated all aspects of Bill's career into strict narratives of black and white. Through such an interpretation, the career of Railroad Bill could be read as a metaphor for black authority run rampant and a justification for an intensified season of persecution. The slippery character and unknown identity of Railroad Bill allowed the famous shape-shifter to emerge and reemerge in various forms, crafted by the tellers of his tale. Lacking a concrete identity for their outlaw, Bill's followers—both literal and otherwise—constructed personas for him that fulfilled their own perceptions, stereotypes, traditions, and needs. Under the social constructions of 1890s Alabama, Railroad Bill's identity merged naturally with its own outward and visible blackness, that measuring stick by which the southern self was compulsively defined. Despite the efforts of a white press to close the curtain on Railroad Bill, his life and death remained a small if representative act in a drama that, at the turn of the twentieth century, had only begun.

NOTES

1. Brewton *Pine Belt News*, 10 March 1896; Montgomery *Daily Advertiser*, 8 March 1896.

2. *Pine Belt News*, 10 March 1896.

3. *Daily Advertiser*, 8 March 1896. The most often-cited synopsis of Railroad Bill's history and legend is Carl Carmer's literary treatment in *Stars Fell on Alabama* (University of Alabama Press, 1934), 122–25. One of the more detailed, if also biased, biographical accounts to appear is former L&N officer J. B. Harlan's "Railroad Bill," *The L. & N. Employes'* [sic] *Magazine*, May 1927, 30–31, 69–70. Two Escambia County newspapers, *The Atmore Advance* and *The Brewton Standard*, gathered many of the original local newspaper items in their bound bicentennial edition, *Heritage 76: A Historical Review of Escambia County and its Communities*, 30 September 1976. Both Norm Cohen, *Long Steel Rail: The Railroad in American Folksong* (University of Illinois Press, 1981), 122–31, and James Penick, "Railroad Bill," *Gulf Coast Historical Review*, 10.1 (1994): 85–92, offer useful historical analyses.

4. "Many Remembered Early Outlaws of this Section," *Atmore Advance*, 3 December 1931; Kay Nuzum, *A History of Baldwin County* (The Baldwin Times, 1971), 123; Marjorie Jagendorf, *Folk Stories of the South* (Vanguard Press, Inc., 1972), 13.

5. *Heritage 76*; *Daily Advertiser*, 5 July 1895, 9 July 1895, 3 August 1895, 7 August 1895; *Pine Belt News*, 6 August 1895.

6. John W. Roberts, *From Trickster to Badman: The Black Folk Hero in Slavery and Freedom* (University of Pennsylvania Press, 1989), 186; H. C. Brearley, "Ba-ad Nigger," *South Atlantic Quarterly*, 38 (1939): 75–81.

7. *Daily Advertiser*, 5 July 1895; *Pine Belt News*, 9 July 1895.

8. *Daily Advertiser*, 5 July 1895; *Pine Belt News*, 9 July 1895.

9. *Daily Advertiser*, 5 July 1895.

10. *Pine Belt News*, 9 July 1895; *Daily Advertiser*, 8 July 1895; *Daily Advertiser*, 11 July 1895.

11. *Daily Advertiser*, 10 July 1895, 11 July 1895, 2 August 1895, 4 August 1895.

12. *Pine Belt News*, 9 July 1895.

13. *Daily Advertiser*, 5 July 1895, 10 July 1895.

14. *Ibid.*, 3 August 1895, 10 July 1895, 1 August 1895, 4 August 1895.

15. *Ibid.*, 9 July 1895.

16. *Pine Belt News*, 16 July 1895; *Daily Advertiser*, 13 August 1895.

17. *Daily Advertiser*, 17 August 1895, 8 March 1896.

18. Eric Hobsbawm, *Bandits* (Pantheon Books, 1969), 58. For more on the role of the badman in black folklore, see, for example, Lawrence Levine, *Black Culture and Black Consciousness* (Oxford University Press, 1977), 407–20.

19. *Daily Advertiser*, 7 August 1895.

20. Albert Murray, *Train Whistle Guitar* (Vintage, 1974), 64.

21. D. K. Wilgus and Eleanor R. Long, "The Blues Ballad and the Genesis of Style in Traditional Narrative Song," in *Narrative Folksong, New Directions: Essays in Appreciation of W. Edson Richmond*, ed. Carol L. Edwards and Kathleen E. B. Manley (Westview Press, 1985) 437–82. Cecelia Conway's discussion of "man-against-the-law songs" in the banjo-song repertoire of Dink Roberts addresses both the role of the outlaw figure in black musical performance and the cre-

ation of meaning within a blues ballad form; see Conway, *African Banjo Echoes in Appalachia: A Study in Folk Traditions* (University of Tennessee Press, 1995), 23–84.

22. Howard W. Odum, "Folk-Song and Folk-Poetry as found in the Secular Songs of the Southern Negroes," *Journal of American Folklore*, 24.93 (1911): 290; Jack and Olivia Solomon, *Sweet Bunch of Daisies: Folk Songs from Alabama* (Colonial Press, 1991), 186, 187; Vera Hall, "Railroad Bill," Library of Congress AFS 1315 B2; MacEdward Leach and Horace P. Beck, "Songs from Rappahannock County, Virginia," *Journal of American Folklore* 63.249 (1969): 280; Will Bennett, "Railroad Bill" (Vocalion 1464), 1929. Reissued on *Sinners and Saints, 1926–1931* (Document 5106), 1992.

23. *Daily Advertiser*, 8 March 1896; *Pine Belt News*, 10 March 1896.

24. *Pine Belt News*, 10 March 1896; Harlan, "Railroad Bill," 70; *Pine Belt News*, 10 March 1896; *Daily Advertiser*, 10 March 1896.

25. See Grace Elizabeth Hale, *Making Whiteness: The Culture of Segregation in the South, 1890–1940* (Random House, 1998) 199–239, and Leon F. Litwack, *Trouble in Mind: Black Southerners in the Age of Jim Crow* (Random House, 1998) for broader discussions of the culture of lynching in the South. For the souvenir-dismemberment of black bodies, see Hale 229–30 and Litwack 296.

26. *Daily Advertiser*, 8 March 1896; *Pine Belt News*, 10 March 1896. The bitterweeds and blood-poisoning legends appear in *Heritage 76*.

27. Norm Cohen describes the sources of public antipathy toward the railroad in his *Long Steel Rail*, 12, 99–109.

Vietnam War Memorial

POETRY BY ROBERT MORGAN

The "black wall uncovered here" stretches "on and on through the ground," ultimately "with all our names" hidden below. A Civil War kinship with Vietnam War dead, courtesy of the collections of the Library of Congress.

What we see first seems a shadow
or a retaining wall in the park,
like half a giant pool or half
an exposed foundation. The names
start a few to the column at
the shallow ends and grow panel
by deeper panel as though month
by month to the point of opposing
planes. From that pit you can't see much
official Washington, just sky
and trees and names and people on
the Mall and the Capitol like
a fancy urn. For this is a wedge
into the earth, a ramp of names
driven into the nation's green,
a black mirror of names many
as the text of a book published
in stone, beginning almost
imperceptibly in the lawn
on one side and growing on black
pages bigger than any reader
(as you look for your own name in
each chapter) and then thin away
like a ledger into turf again,
with no beginning, no end. As though
the black wall uncovered here a few
rods for sunlight and recognition
runs on and on through the ground in
both directions, with all our names
on the hidden panels, while
these names shine in the open noon.

Ed. note: This poem was originally published in Robert Morgan's Sigodlin *(Wesleyan University Press) and will be included in his* New and Selected Poems, *which will appear in Spring 2004 from LSU Press.*

Not Forgotten

Southern Nigerian

BY ELAINE NEIL ORR

"When I was a small girl in Nigeria, my father, after his 'rest time,' would sometimes push my sister, Becky, and me on the swing set before he headed back to his job as business manager at the hospital. 'Here we go to Sycamore Town,' he sang over and over, his agile arms giving one daughter a push and then the other." In her father's arms, Elaine Neil Orr, with her mother and sister Becky in front of their first home in Ogbomosho, in southern Nigeria, courtesy of the author.

91

When I was a small girl in Nigeria, my father, after his "rest time," would sometimes push my sister, Becky, and me on the swing set before he headed back to
his job as business manager at the hospital. "Here we go to Sycamore Town," he
sang over and over, his agile arms giving one daughter a push and then the other.
"Here we go to Sycamore Town." For a long while I didn't wonder what the lyric
meant, no more than I wondered about "here we go round the mulberry bush"
when there was no mulberry bush to go round. But at some point, Becky or I
must have asked and then the story was revealed; Sycamore is a small village close
to the South Carolina hamlet of Fairfax where my mother was born and my parents, Annie Lee Thomas and Lloyd Houston Neil, fell in love. So while American
youth were imagining a trek to the African metropolis of Timbuktu, I was being
summoned to the fabulous American outpost of Sycamore.

Much later, my father told me that on our first furlough, before I was old
enough to remember, he was approached by an old-timer in Fairfax who advised
him to *take all these niggers back with you to Africa.* That was 1956, the year Flannery
O'Connor's "Greenleaf" appeared in *Kenyon Review.* My father never called anyone "nigger" and no one in our house ever called anyone stupid. It was forbid-
den. I heard "nigger" only in the United States. Still, I was a white southerner in

*"A partially wooded savannah region, Yoruba land was for me a distinct if complex South full of crossroads:
churches and shrines, market women and Nigerian doctors, family portraits and the talking drum. It was not
to be confused with northern Nigeria, the home of the Hausa-Fulani and the shrouded god Allah." Elaine
Neil Orr (left) with her mother (center) and a missionary aunt, who are preparing refreshments for a Nigerian
Women's Missionary Union meeting in Eku. The Orrs' Chevy wagon sits in the background.*

Nigeria because my parents were Southern Baptist medical missionaries from South Carolina.

But that's only half of the story. I was also southern *Nigerian* because my family and I were nestled in the heart of the Yoruba nation, in the town of Ogbomosho, in southern Nigeria. This is important. It means I was and am in many ways a southerner. A partially wooded savannah region, Yoruba land was for me a distinct if complex South full of crossroads: churches and shrines, market women and Nigerian doctors, family portraits and the talking drum. It was not to be confused with northern Nigeria, the home of the Hausa-Fulani and the shrouded god Allah.

To this land of palms, my parents brought dreams of southern living. My mother's early life retained the residue of southern aristocracy, and my father was the son of a Baptist preacher. In this way I was reared in a bouquet of southern culture, but in my case it's hard to know which South came first. Certainly, I was perplexed by the American South I knew on furloughs, once I began paying attention. Here I found a queer country of white abundance and settled weariness and no Africans. I don't mean no black people. There were black people; there just weren't any Africans.

"To this land of palms, my parents brought dreams of southern living. My mother's early life retained the residue of southern aristocracy, and my father was the son of a Baptist preacher. In this way I was reared in a bouquet of southern culture, but in my case it's hard to know which South came first."
The girls' dorm at Newton Memorial School in Oshogbo, where Elaine Neil Orr attended beginning in sixth grade.

"I have always thought my origin is Ogbomosho, the dusty Yoruba town where I was born in 1954. What I most recall is the sun slamming down, ricocheting off tin roofs of mud and plaster houses that duplicated one another endlessly down a thousand bicycle paths, splashes of puddles during the rains, and a hundred women on their way to market." The author's birthplace in Ogbomosho.

I have always thought my origin is Ogbomosho, the dusty Yoruba town where I was born in 1954. What I most recall is the sun slamming down, ricocheting off tin roofs of mud and plaster houses that duplicated one another endlessly down a thousand bicycle paths, splashes of puddles during the rains, and a hundred women on their way to market. The laterite road was elevated so that perching on the seat of our sierra-gold 1957 Chevrolet station wagon, my face was level with the faces of people in front of their shops. Everything looked brown except for the cloth. The cloth was blue, blue, and more blue, enough blue to have left the sky in debt. The women and the men wore the cloth. Many of the children wore only bracelets or low-slung shorts or a wrap.

At the Mobil station where my father fills the tank with petrol, I ponder the lifting wings of Pegasus the horse on the side of the building. I have never seen a horse, rather goats and Brahman cattle and chickens in the road and black mambas and red-headed lizards and all manner of birds, including hawks, and once, before a missionary nurse shot it, a monitor lizard in my front yard. My reverie is interrupted when a boy my sister's age thrusts a tray of Trebor Mints and chewing gum in little rectangular packets through the window. "Buy chewing gum," he instructs loudly, emphasizing the word gum, as if I might not understand English. "Buy chewing gum." He does not step back or retreat. When my father reenters our vehicle, he digs for ages in his shorts pocket before producing the three pence for the purchase. He stages this elongated transaction as a kind of improvisational comedy and it works. The boy and I both laugh, though perhaps for different reasons.

"A gardener carried water for the evening's baths, and we all used the same water: first Becky and me, then my mother, then my father. In spite of these 'hardships,' it is not difficult to see that my mother's life in West Africa allowed a return to certain privileges of her grandmother's life in Carolina. She might have bathed in tepid water, but someone else had drawn it." Elaine Neil Orr and her parents (far left), with a Nigerian marriage party.

Three major ethnic groups and hundreds of other "minor" ones inhabit modern Nigeria. The big three are the Yoruba, the Igbo, and the Hausa-Fulani. In my earliest years, I imagined that Yoruba land encompassed most of the country. The arid territory of the huge northern region was diminished in my mind by its absence from my experience. I knew of it primarily through Fulani herders on the road with their great horned cattle, headed south to market, and Hausa traders, tall elegant men who brought beautiful works of art to sell to the missionaries, laying out their wares on mats on the veranda and praying to Allah as regularly as the hibiscus that opened in the morning and closed in the late afternoon. As far as I was concerned, they were all foreigners. When I was older I tried without success to convert some Hausa traders to Christianity, hoping to pull them into the green pastures of our southern world, but they refused "twelve steps to salvation."

The British established the Northern and Southern Protectorates of what would become Nigeria after the Berlin Conference of 1885. The two were amalgamated in 1914 when Nigeria was officially launched. The British always preferred the North because the aristocratic emirs provided such a fine resource for indirect rule. Here one ruled by ruling the rulers who then ruled the people. Governance in the South was messier because the Yoruba and Igbo were more independent-minded. As Nigerian nationalism grew following World War II, one Sir Arthur Richards proposed a constitution that included three regional councils: the West (Yoruba) and the East (Igbo) in the South, with the North (Hausa-Fulani) remaining intact. Thus two figures for dividing Nigeria hover over its twentieth century: the North/South line and the tripartite lines of West/East/North. I felt the shadow of both of these figures growing up. With my family I lived in the southwest and traveled the roads into the southeast and back. Once only did we venture north to Jos, our car lifting to the plateau where we would need sweaters until midday, the Nigerian huts were round, not square, and there were hardly any palms. In the North, I discovered an apparently *real* horse but in truth, I thought, *this is a land of phantoms and myths.*

When the British bowed out in 1960, they left a legacy of representation based on population, a system that favored the larger North. Even if the South were united (Yoruba and Igbo and a myriad of minorities), it would always have fewer votes. When the civil war arrived in my teen-age years, flying in from the Bight of Biafra like a huge bat on a motorcycle, the cause could be traced to the British-installed pattern of regionalism and northern dominance. Even today, with some northern states instituting Sharia law, the fighting continues. I have always favored the South and the West, and in this sense I am a true daughter of Yoruba land. The staff at the Ogbomosho hospital gave me the name Bamidele, *follow me home,* and even today when I consider "home," it is an Ogbomosho house I see, present as a god and as powerful, round and deep and colored in its fullness, a globed thing, an entire universe.

DREAMS OF SOUTHERN LIVING

Along with the lingerie, dresses, shoes, and cosmetics assembled for her first tour, my mother packed books of instruction produced by American makers of drapery fabric. In Nigeria in a Lagos market she found a suitable fabric featuring ivory roses, never mind that our tropical gardens produced frangipani and caladium. To hold the draperies so they hung evenly, she sewed English shillings into the corners of each panel. I would pay dearly today to recover those window dressings my mother dreamed of aboard the *African Patriot*, the freighter she and my father and my sister crossed over on.

Even with those fine drapes, we had no running water in our first house. A gar-

"Later, we moved to the first home I remember, a bungalow located on the high point of the compound. My first remembered Christmas was in that house. I recall waking before dawn and hearing a chorus of angels on the front porch singing through the screens: Jo-y to de weld *with the most beautiful Nigerian accent. My father was with the nursing students, but their voices drowned his out." The author returns to her first remembered home.*

dener carried water for the evening's baths, and we all used the same water: first Becky and me, then my mother, then my father. In spite of these "hardships," it is not difficult to see that my mother's life in West Africa allowed a return to certain privileges of her grandmother's life in Carolina. She might have bathed in tepid water, but someone else had drawn it.

Later, we moved to the first home I remember, a bungalow located on the high point of the compound. My first remembered Christmas was in that house. I recall waking before dawn and hearing a chorus of angels on the front porch singing through the screens: *Jo-y to de weld* with the most beautiful Nigerian accent. My father was with the nursing students but their voices drowned his out.

In many ways, we were the typical southern American family in our three bedroom house, with our station wagon and our swing set and, believe it or not, our cocker spaniel. In my present life, I spot the same bungalow design in older North Carolina neighborhoods—well, with some modifications. The windows were louvered and covered with both screen and a heavy metal latticing; the floors were finished with tile, no carpet; we had a towering water tank in the back yard, and all the building blocks were concrete.

As I remember, my mother's interior decorating did not end with window dressings; she "followed through" (my father's instruction on how to hit a tennis ball) in home decor. Never was it that our furniture lined up against the walls, as in some missionary homes. My mother knew how to create clustered areas, thematic moments in a room.

First the piano, that majestic piece to which all other furniture bowed. Here it is to the left as you enter the living room through the screened door from the porch, a slight breeze fanning you inward. Yes, the piano, upon which rests the brass lamp with its ivory shade, drawing out of the wood a monochromatic medley of calm golds and browns. If I turn to my right, there are the mission chairs that followed me through my Nigerian life like double first cousins. Built by Mr. Bolarinwa and his staff of Yoruba carpenters at the hospital, they sit at a forty-five degree angle, their cushions newly covered in green fabric because my mother's colors are always blue and green with accents of lavender, the colors of the hydrangea in her mother's South Carolina garden. Within the angle, the beloved square table whose surface is an infinitely precious design of various inlaid woods. And upon it recent copies of National Geographic *arranged like an open fan. Here also the turntable out of which spins the Chopin sonata I will play years later in my eighth grade recital. And the radio. Here my parents sit at night after I am asleep. I did not see them then, but now I come out into the hallway and watch my mother reading* The African Awakening *by Basil Davidson and my father tipping to the left, his ear reaching for the sound of* The Voice of America. *Perhaps he will hear mention of his beloved Clemson Tigers.*

Across from that cluster, the couch and in front of it—my mother's one nod to West African furnishings—the tim tims, those prized stuffed leather stools of my childhood, their tops a mosaic of woven dyed "threads." On the wall, pictures hang in groups—and not too high: "They should meet your eye when you stand," my mother says, referring in reality to another home on the compound in which you have to assume the posture of star gazing in order to see framed prints.

Our dinner table, a mahogany opera, was also built by those Yoruba craftsmen at the carpenters' shop. They built most of our furniture. All my mother had to do was select a photograph of some coveted piece from *Better Homes and Gardens* and those men could make it. Before meals, that table was set for us—just as in South Carolina my mother's mother had someone lay her table. At dinner, served midday, we partook of fried chicken and saintly lima beans and mashed potatoes and, our one local food, sliced mangos. Early I learned the sacredness of "May I be excused, please" and the value of decorative flowers: marigolds in a cut glass vase, zinnias in a tall cylinder, a single red hibiscus in a low bowl. These were my mother's poems.

Always I believed that my family was of a slightly higher class than other missionaries, and in my thinking I reflected my parents' sense of southern aristocracy. Our living room was decorated tastefully and we used real silverware every day. Every meal, even breakfast, was formally served. Our car was newer; our toys at Christmas were the best; my father won many a tennis tournament. When my mother spoke, people listened.

"Always I believed that my family was of a slightly higher class than other missionaries, and in my thinking I reflected my parents' sense of southern aristocracy." The author (second from right, back) and her mother (center, back) with friends in Eku.

SOUTHERN NIGERIAN HOSPITALITY

Running about that Ogbomosho bungalow on an average day with my father at work and my mother sometimes home, sometimes teaching, and Becky, the socialite, out calling on friends, my constellation of human contact was made up primarily of Abike and our cooks, first Ishola and then Sam and later Abraham. My parents kept sending the young men to school so that they worked themselves out of help almost as soon as they got it.

Abike was my mainstay, toting me to my first schoolroom: the guava tree grove. Here I heard gods calling: *the road does not need lies; the meek shall inherit the earth.* It was Abike who called me back to the living that time I fell on the hard cement floor of our porch and was knocked unconscious. I recall her application of Band-aids on numerous, less dramatic occasions. I sat on the toilet seat while she washed the minor wound, instructing me: *Be quiet'O. You're a big gyl.* Then she pressed the Band-aid on and pulled me back to my feet in one robust movement. In the mornings she helped me dress, her fingers slender and cool. I was silent when she touched me out of respect for her hands, even though I was annoyed by any prickliness in the seams of my clothing and often despaired that my socks did not feel pulled up sufficiently.

Once I sharpened all of my crayons until there was nothing but a fluffy pile. *Ee-lane, what ah you do-en?* she demanded. But then she rather casually cleared the

"Running about that Ogbomosho bungalow on an average day with my father at work and my mother sometimes home, sometimes teaching, and Becky, the socialite, out calling on friends, my constellation of human contact was made up primarily of Abike and our cooks, first Ishola and then Sam and later Abraham. My parents kept sending the young men to school so that they worked themselves out of help almost as soon as they got it." The author (second from left, front) with her family and Ishola Kunle's family in front of her first Ogbomosho home.

table with the aid of a nearby trashcan. She and Sam laughed at me in unison when she supplied me with a huge glass of water, which I called *l'adel l'adel*, because I swallowed with such eagerness my throat sounded toadish with each gulp.

I did not know that I remembered Ishola until recently, when I recovered an old photograph. Now I see that his face is older in memory than my own, with his ebony skin and his almost damaging smile—it caused such self-doubt in others—and what were to me the beautiful feathers across his cheeks. Sam was a petite man, and Abraham was large and imposing in stature like the Old Testament prophet. Abraham's face was full of drama, but Sam's was like the evening, calm and abiding, like that hymn *Abide with me: fast falls the eventide*. On workdays, these young men wore European-style, short-sleeved shirts, but they were localized by being cut very large and thus made airy and cool. There was something beautiful and gentlemanly in the bearing of these men in their clothes.

On Sundays, in church, Abraham was dressed in Yoruba attire: an embroidered, loose tunic that fell to below the knees and marvelous sleeves folded back over the shoulders, flowing trousers that made themselves close at the ankle, along with sunglasses and a carved walking stick, though he was only eighteen or nineteen.

One thing that's true about southern Nigerians is that they are happy to show you they have enough of a thing. For example, they put yards and yards of fabric into their traditional clothing, nothing like the tailored look Americans prefer. Such clothes are like jewelry: the more and the bigger the better. If Yoruba parents have many children, they bring all of them to salute you, as Ishola once did on Christmas Eve, toting his four offspring, all of them handsome and well dressed as if they were on their way to a wedding. And if you dine with a Yoruba couple, they provide enough food for an entire village, if they have it to give. Nigerians believe in plenty.

Even those who have "small small" will hope to give you something, for example, a voluminous greeting. Nigerians don't say "hi."

> *E kaaro, se alaafia ni o?* Good morning, how are you?
> *E kaaro, a dupe.* Good morning. I am well.
> *Ile nko?* How is your house?
> *O wa.* It is fine.
> *Oga nko?* How about your husband?
> *O wa.* He is fine.
> *Omo nko?* How are your children?
> *O wa.* They are fine.

My mother says that she did not understand Paul's injunction to the early churches *not to spend too much time greeting the brethren* until she reached Nigeria. But even Yoruba *Christians* will not be corrected by Paul on the point of terrific hellos, for they are above all hospitable.

"The first white missionary to visit Ibadan was given a hog and twenty thousand cowries (a pound sterling at the time) on his arrival. When he indicated that the gift was too rich, the chief simply responded that if the missionary complained again, he would have to double the amount. Thinking about this cultural trait leads me to wonder if what we think of as southern hospitality may be southern Nigerian *hospitality brought over on slave ships." The author with American and Nigerian friends.*

This sociability may have been their Achilles heel with the British and with us; nevertheless Yoruba generosity was a governing element in the South of my youth. The first white missionary to visit Ibadan was given a hog and twenty thousand cowries (a pound sterling at the time) on his arrival. When he indicated that the gift was too rich, the chief simply responded that if the missionary complained again, he would have to double the amount. Thinking about this cultural trait leads me to wonder if what we think of as southern hospitality may be southern *Nigerian* hospitality brought over on slave ships. Certainly in Nigeria such hospitality is not self-effacing. It elevates the giver, showing his or her power to give. If you look at traditional Yoruba religious sayings you can see that kindness and generosity are great virtues and that they are linked with wealth. Those who are kind have the unfailing blessing of Olodumare, God the Creator: Thus,

> The calabash of the kind breaks not.
> The dish of the kind splits not.
> It is both money and children that flow into the house of the kind.

"Of our second furlough in Winston-Salem, North Carolina, in 1960, I can report that most everything was white. The Baptist church we attended was so white I needed sunglasses, like Abraham. I had never seen so many white people. I saw some brown people, but they were not Africans. They did not come up to my mother on the street, their arms in flight, their voices lifting into the air and bursting like rain clouds as they grasped her hands and greeted her." Coming to America in 1960, the author (left) with her family in Greenville, South Carolina.

Ishola already had his beautiful children as proof, and later Abike married a wealthy man. And Sam became a pharmacist, and Abraham became a famous actor, traveling to Europe and the United States.

SWEET BUT NOT SATISFYING

Of our second furlough in Winston-Salem, North Carolina, in 1960, I can report that most everything was white. The Baptist church we attended was so white I needed sunglasses, like Abraham. All the people were white; the walls were white; in fact the walls were so white I thought the paint was still wet and skimmed like a tight-rope walker down the centers of rooms and hallways. I had never seen so many white people. I witnessed the movie *The Snow Queen*, or was it *The Ice Queen*? I can't remember that, but I do remember loads and loads of sleet that year falling on our borrowed lawn. I attended first grade in a trailer because the elementary school was brimming over—the baby-boom generation. I saw some brown people, but they were not Africans. They did not come up to my mother on the street, their arms in flight, their voices lifting into the air and bursting like rain clouds as they grasped her hands and greeted her. Instead, the elderly men in overalls walking along the sides of roads seemed to have lost their brio.

Many things in the American South were sweet but not satisfying: the cherry Cokes we bought at the corner store, chewing gums out of round machines, the

"In my life in West Africa, I faced the same crises and anxieties that attend any growing up. But I hardly knew what was going on around me. Only as I began to write about my early life did I begin to piece together all of the fragments, tails of stories, that went into making me southern in Nigeria." Snapshot of modern-day Ogbomosho, courtesy of the author.

plastic-looking narcissus that sprang up after all that sleet, summer peaches—which were fine as far as they went but they did not go far enough, not as far as a mango, whose palate is deep as graves. I sat rocking on my grandmother's porch, looking out at all those azaleas and wondered about the news that I had a *real* family here while my missionary aunts and uncles were apparently pretend.

In my life in West Africa, I faced the same crises and anxieties that attend any growing up. But I hardly knew what was going on around me. I held a multitude of things in my heart, and they multiplied down endless compound paths. But I had little understanding of the vast trade winds that had swept the Lloyd Neils up out of Fairfax and deposited them at the Gulf of Guinea. Only as I began to write about my early life did I begin to piece together all of the fragments, tails of stories, that went into making me southern in Nigeria. A vital piece is my mother's family's ownership of slaves in the American South before the Civil War. I had learned vaguely about this history as a young adult, but I had not seen how this piece wove so intimately together the two Souths of my childhood, indeed the *neighborhoods* of my growing up.

This is how I recognized that intimacy.

As I am doing research for my memoirs, I find in a book a picture of the Ethiope River, the

"I have come to believe that I am as much African as American. I am bound to two Souths like a huge cresting arch." On a return trip to southern Nigeria the author visits with a hospital administrator (center), who has her father's old job and "knows" him because he has seen his signature, and a seminary professor (right), whom she knew in her youth as a babysitter for another missionary family.

cold, clear, given-from-god river I swam in as a girl, with white sandy bottom and booming vegetation surrounding it and fish of neon colors. This photograph is a true diviner's text. In the center I see the mighty logs—two or three huge mahoganies and irokos, trimmed of branches and roots, almost perfect cylinders, attached parallel in sets of two or three—which I often witnessed gliding down river, directed by a lone driver. I would dive out from the pier and hoist myself onto the great raft for a lift down to the next landing. I recognize the way the logs are tied together as they make their heavy and inevitable way to market. I can even feel those cool slick trunks. Their destination: Sapele. But Sapele brings Warri to mind, because it was equidistant from my home at the time, the village of Eku in the Midwest region, and because we took turns going to either city to shop. And as I continue to read about the area I make a discovery: Warri was a slave-trading station in the eighteenth and early nineteenth centuries. When I look at a map of Africa and the Americas in African History in Maps, *I recognize an awful symmetry that rewrites my family history. A heavy black line connects the Nigerian coast with Charleston, South Carolina, the arrows pointing like the hand of God from one South to another. What this means, the map key instructs, is that Africans were being exported from places like the mouth of the Ethiope through the West Indies and finally into places like my mother's grandmother's backyard. The Ethiope is named for the first colonial boat that chugged up that tight current. Perhaps members of extended families of Nigerians I had met as a girl had been bound like those logs traveling down that swift stream.*

My mother grew up with "Aunt Hale," an ex-slave who worked for her family. She remembers also "Aunt Fibbie," another ex-slave and mulatto who was the intimate friend of her grandmother, Mary Rebecca Harter Deer. Indeed, my mother has long suspected that Aunt Fibbie and Mary Rebecca were half sisters. Did my great, great grandfather purchase slaves from the Nigerian coast? Could Aunt Fibbie have had Yoruba ancestry?

I venture to say that my family's first contact with Nigeria was by boat, but not the African Patriot. *Contact may have begun much earlier. And I think this history is why my mother was compelled at an early age to become a missionary and why she and my father ended up in Africa, and not just Africa but Nigeria, and not just Nigeria, but the Nigerian South.*

I have come to believe that I am as much African as American in spite of my whiteness. In both cases, however, I am distinctively southern. As such, I participate in a great web of national and international histories as well as personal ones. I am bound to two Souths like a huge cresting arch. On the other hand, and in another way, I belong to neither coast. I drift somewhere in the tepid mid-Atlantic. And still I claim for myself one location, one South: the accidental, purposeful, peculiar South of my beginnings in that Ogbomosho bungalow, in those southern gardens of the guava tree, in the night market, in the voice of Abike, in the blues and greens of our living room, in the sandy veil of dry-season air, even in the arms of the Ethiope, that daring cross of a river.

Editors' Note: Read more about Elaine Orr in her memoir, Gods of Noonday: A White Girl's African Life, *published by the University of Virginia Press.*

books

South to the Future

An American Region in the
Twenty-first Century
Edited by Fred Hobson
Mercer University Lamar Memorial Lectures,
Number 44
The University of Georgia Press, 2002
108 pp. Cloth $24.95

Reviewed by **Michael Kreyling**, professor of
English at Vanderbilt University and author of *Inventing
Southern Literature*, published by the University Press of
Mississippi in 1999.

Georgia, like all southern states, boasts its own traditions. In April there is the
Masters, where broadcast money is less important than the exquisite pleasures of
total control of the event, where the field is restricted, where elderly white gen-
tlemen with first names like Hootie talk about golf shots of yore, and where see-
ing the front nine of Augusta National on television is headline news. In the fall
there is the Mercer University Lamar Memorial Lecture Series. With forty-four
repetitions, the Lamar Lectures are twenty-three years junior to the Masters. But
the hold of "tradition" is no less authoritative.

Introductions to serial volumes, like announcements from the first tee, stress
continuity, reminding the reader of the champions of the past who have traversed
the course: Donald Davidson (the inaugural lecturer—the Bobby Jones of the series), Cleanth Brooks, Walter Sullivan, Lewis Simpson—a roster of the Gene
Sarazens, Arnold Palmers, and Slammin' Sammy Sneads of southern literary crit-
icism and history. The benefactress of the Lamar Lectures is "Dolly" Blount
Lamar, superbly connected by birth and marriage to the elite of the South when
the upper-case "S" was automatic. Eugenia Dorothy Blount Lamar (1867–1955)
was a daughter of the South reared in the furnace of Reconstruction. She was
Southern Conservatism to the backbone—the kind of antimodern, antiprogres-
sive, static "drag" that Gunnar Myrdal and his ilk loved to hate. President-General
of the Georgia Division of the United Daughters of the Confederacy, Mrs. Lamar
resisted change as she would have resisted Sherman. She spoke out to the Georgia legislature against votes for women, warning the men that extending the fran-
chise to women would jeopardize white political control. At the premier of

Selznick's *Gone With the Wind* in 1939, she averred that the film was absolutely true to historical fact. Although she died before the first lecture, it is safe to bet that she would have approved of the choice of Donald Davidson in 1957.

One wonders, though, what Dolly would have made of the millennium volume. To acknowledge the new age, the Lamar Lectures committee changed the format from individual lecturer to a symposium. Fred Hobson, editor of No. 44, claims that "change [is] the keynote of these lectures." "If one is looking for a revolutionary age in the U.S. South," he continues, "it is upon us, and the essays in this volume wrestle mightily with its perils and its promise." But tradition holds its own against revolution. The editor and three of the contributors have deep University of North Carolina at Chapel Hill connections: Hobson, Linda Wagner-Martin, and Joel Williamson are professors there. Thadious Davis is a former member of the faculty. Randall Kenan, whose work is the subject of half of Davis's stylish and provocative essay, is a graduate. As with Augusta National, new members to the club are scarce. Many potential members are named in the introduction and in some of the essays—as leading platoons of cultural critics in the "revolutionary age"—but in the essays themselves one more often encounters old duffers like C. Vann Woodward and W. J. Cash.

Suspicion of the new runs deep in this symposium. Only Davis seems happy to break the hegemony of traditional canons of genre and of the critic's voice and function. Williamson's essay takes up Woodward's venerable attempt to explain the Southern Renaissance, and seems content with the master's understanding of novelists as enigmatic as wizards and their works as mysteries quite separate from the world historians deal with. Edward Ayers, a historian of the South also quite haunted by Woodward, closes the volume with an imaginative monologue by a Generation X'er extrapolated to 2076. "The Inevitable Future of the South," according to Ayers, is to be "consolidated" by interstates, franchises, homogenized but still Protestant religion—all distinctiveness snuffed out or paved over. So much for "promise": Davidson's Leviathan triumphs after all in a suburban "Blade Runner" South.

Maybe "change" has become the norm: we've become jaded by diversity. When Tiger Woods (whose presence at Augusta swinging a club rather than carrying a bag changed golf—and Fuzzy Zoeller's career) won his third green jacket in April of 2002, golf writers complained that the competition had given up. The 2000 Lamar Lectures committee failed to think outside club boundaries. Hobson ticked off a pair of names of the southern voices of the twenty-first century: Barbara Ladd, Deborah Cohn. There are others: Scott Romine, Patricia Yaeger, Jacquelyn Hall, Grace Elizabeth Hale, Susan Donaldson and Anne Goodwyn Jones and the contributors to their volume of essays, *Haunted Bodies*. A Symposium with some of these people participating would have shaken Dolly in her grave.

Hill Folks

A History of Arkansas
Ozarkers and Their Image
By Brooks Blevins
University of North Carolina Press, 2002
340 pp. Cloth $55.00; paper $19.95

Reviewed by **John C. Inscoe**, professor of history
at the University of Georgia and author of numerous
works on nineteenth-century Appalachia, including *The
Heart of Confederate Appalachia: Western North Carolina's
Civil War*, coauthored with Gordon B. McKinney.

The Ozarks have long suffered from an image problem. Even compared with
Appalachia—itself no stranger to degrading stereotypes and blatant misrepresen-
tation—these other southern highlands have been exceptionally maligned. One
of the region's few definitive studies, folklorist Vance Randolph's *The Ozarks*, was
tellingly subtitled *An American Survival of Primitive Society*; he pronounced the area
one of the "the most backward and deliberately unprogressive regions of the
United States."

Unlike Appalachia though, the Ozarks have also suffered from scholarly ne-
glect. In the past couple of decades, Appalachian scholars have produced a remarkable outpouring of work on that region's history, culture, literature, and environment. The Ozarks, on the other hand, have inspired nothing comparable, at
least until now. Brooks Blevins, a native of the region, has begun to fill the relative void with *Hill Folks*, a comprehensive history of one section of the Ozarks—
those that extend across northwestern and north central Arkansas. (Missouri
claims the majority of the range, and Oklahoma a much smaller section of it.) As
rich as Blevins's historical narrative is—a well-written blend of economic, social,
and cultural history—it is the added layer of analysis on changing perceptions of
the region and its people that most distinguishes his study.

The Ozarks' past makes for a somewhat more compact history than that of
Appalachia. Only in the early-nineteenth century did serious settlement begin
there, though, curiously, the fertile Springfield Plain in Arkansas's northwestern-
most corner had already emerged as the most populous and prosperous area in
the state when it entered the Union in 1836. Also unlike any other highland region, cotton came to dominate the cash economy for some of the hill folk, although it emerged too late to provide them with the prosperity or affluence that
it did for antebellum lowland plantation areas.

The so-called "discovery" of the Ozarks by outsiders took place well after that of the Appalachians. Whereas those more eastern highlanders faced transformative forces—the influx of mining and timber companies, missionaries and social workers, railroads, and tourists—during the post–Civil War decades, similar developments came somewhat later to the Arkansas highlands, sometimes as late as the 1920s and 1930s. Those who did discover the region, according to Blevins, did so with a far more clinical detachment than was true of the missionary zeal and cultural intervention that so characterized the earlier discovery of the Appalachians and their residents.

Midwesterners discovered the curative power of Ozark mineral springs well before the turn of the century, although it was only in the 1920s that the most successful summer resorts came into their own, usually financed and managed by outsiders. More pervasive was the influx of back-to-the-landers—those of the urban middle class who were attracted to the picturesque and remote Ozarks, where they sought to duplicate the simplicity of frontier life with log homes and self-sufficient lifestyles. This romantic sense of "homesteading" reached its height during the Great Depression, when the backwoods became for many "a world foreign to advertising, and sales luring, and trade slogans, and patched pavements."

Blevins notes the irony in the fact that such idyllic notions of the region were being firmly implanted just as its agricultural base and social structure were undergoing major modernizing alterations. A massive outmigration of farm families was followed by yet another influx of midwestern and northern vacationers and retirees, which have made tourism a more dominant part of the region's identity and economic base. The book is at its best in chronicling the contrasts and contradictions of the post–World War II era. Blevins juxtaposes the backgrounds of Ozark natives J. William Fulbright and Orval Faubus to illustrate the region's socio-economic diversity: the Senate's foreign-relations leader's affluent upbringing in the college town of Fayetteville, and the segregation governor's coming of age on a semi-subsistent hillside farm in "comfortable poverty." The business opportunities nurtured in this hill country are also striking: two Fortune 500 companies—Wal-Mart and the Tyson chicken empire—along with the nation's largest trucking company, all began and remain based in the Arkansas Ozarks.

While the Ozarks remain one of the most rural—and whitest—regions of the country, Blevins's fine book demonstrates that these hill folks have experienced far more change and embrace far more socio-economic diversity than the image-makers, both within or without, have acknowledged. In demonstrating that wide discrepancy between image and reality and the reasons behind it, he tells us much not just about the Ozarks, but about the broader dimensions of the interplay between southern culture and regional identity.

About the Contributors

William R. Ferris is the Joel R. Williamson Distinguished Professor of History, Senior Associate Director of the Center for the Study of the American South, and adjunct professor of folklore at The University of North Carolina at Chapel Hill. Former chairman of the National Endowment for the Humanities, he has made numerous documentary films and authored over 100 publications in the fields of folklore, history, literature, and photography.

Larry J. Griffin is a professor of sociology and history at Vanderbilt University and is also affiliated with the university's African American program and its American and Southern Studies program. He is beginning a study of southern whites' memories of the Jim Crow era, and is interested in its lingering effects of responsibility, shame, or guilt.

Barbara Hahn has an essay forthcoming in the *Journal of Urban History* and is a doctoral candidate in history at The University of North Carolina at Chapel Hill, where she is completing her dissertation on the technologies of tobacco production.

Burgin Mathews is a graduate student in folklore at the University of North Carolina at Chapel Hill. He served as intern at the Alabama Center for Traditional Culture and has contributed to the *All Music Guide*. He also is the co-founder of *Speak*, a magazine of oral histories in western North Carolina.

Robert Morgan is Kappa Alpha Professor of English at Cornell University and the author of numerous volumes of poetry and fiction. He has received the James B. Hanes Poetry Prize and the North Carolina Award in Literature, as well as Guggenheim, Rockefeller, and National Endowment for the Arts fellowships for his work. *Kirkus Reviews* has called him the "poet laureate of Appalachia."

Elaine Neil Orr holds a Ph.D. in Literature and Theology from Emory University and teaches at North Carolina State University. She received a North Carolina Arts Council Fellowship in creative non-fiction and her memoir, *Gods of Noonday: A White Girl's African Life*, was published by the University of Virginia Press.

John Shelton Reed was the William Rand Kenan Jr. Professor of Sociology and the director of the Odum Institute for Research in Social Science at The University of North Carolina at Chapel Hill. Among his recent books is *1001 Things Everyone Should Know About the South*, written with his wife, Dale Volberg Reed. He is coeditor of *Southern Cultures*.

Ashley B. Thompson is a graduate student in the department of sociology at Vanderbilt University. Her dissertation research deals with the use of photography in studying stigma and identity among the homeless.

Harry L. Watson is a professor of history at The University of North Carolina at Chapel Hill and director of UNC's Center for the Study of the American South. His publications include *Liberty and Power: The Politics of Jacksonian America*, published by Hill & Wang. He also is coeditor of *Southern Cultures*.

The Program on Southern Politics, Media and Public Life

connects the South's leaders to the intellectual resources of the University of North Carolina at Chapel Hill. Through its work, the Program cultivates a patch of common ground where decision makers and opinion shapers debate and discuss trends and issues, ethics and democratic governance.

A part of the Center for the Study of the American South, the Program sponsors the following projects and publications:

- Executive Seminar for Southern Legislators – A retreat for state legislators.

- Southern Journalists Roundtables – Policy and political discussions among reporters, editors and scholars.

- *SouthNow* – A publication covering Southern political trends.

- *North Carolina DataNet* – A newsletter devoted to North Carolina politics.

- *SouthNow Update* – An electronic publication covering public policy developments.

- SouthNow.org – An online source of election data.

Funding for the Program's activities comes from the Z. Smith Reynolds Foundation, Progress Energy and the University of North Carolina at Chapel Hill.

To subscribe to the Program's free publications or learn more about upcoming events, email **southnow@unc.edu**, visit **www.southnow.org** or call **(919) 843–8174.**

Program on Southern Politics, Media and Public Life
Center for the Study of the American South
The University of North Carolina at Chapel Hill
CB# 3365
Chapel Hill, NC 27599-3365

Ferrel Guillory
Director

Thad Beyle
Associate Director

John Quinterno
Assistant Director

Program on Southern Politics, Media and Public Life

"A wonderful book you have to read to believe."

Toi Derricotte, author of *The Black Notebooks*

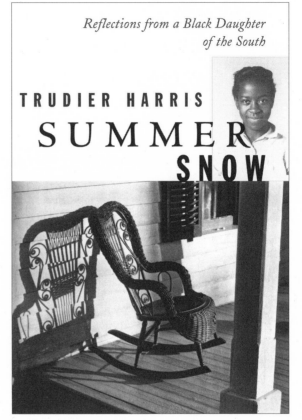

Reflections from a Black Daughter of the South

TRUDIER HARRIS

SUMMER SNOW

$24.00 / hardcover

Summer Snow
Reflections from a Black Daughter of the South
Trudier Harris

A wide-ranging, spirited collection of personal essays about growing up black and Southern

"Noon can be as blinding as midnight; snow no less than sun can cause a vision distortion. Like Zora Neale Hurston, another great daughter of the South, Harris lets her vision be tempered by her love. And make no mistake, the South of Black Americans is a love story. *Summer Snow* reminds us of that … causes us to remember that … lets us celebrate that." —Nikki Giovanni

"Stimulating and provocative, *Summer Snow* resonates with folkloric energy and vividly evocative prose. Trudier Harris's presence and voice vibrate through this journey, guiding her reader with the sheer force of her rigor, grace, and intelligence as well as a goodly amount of wry humor and wit. A reader's dream-book, reminding us all of the resonant claim of southern spaces." —Karla Holloway, author of *Passed On*

BEACON
150

Beacon Press   www.beacon.org

Might as well get *Southern Cultures* the easy way. Subscribe now and save over 35%.

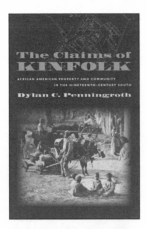
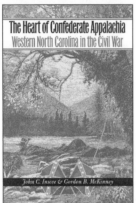

A leading figure in the Tryon artists' colony, George Aid was one of many expatriates in Europe who returned to America after the First World War. Highly regarded on both sides of the Atlantic for his superb printmaking, and a friend of important Impressionists in Paris, he was Northern by birth and Southern by choice. A prototypical artist of the early twentieth century, Aid represents the new wave of cosmopolitanism that invigorated the South's art scene between the world wars.

Why he chose to settle in the North Carolina mountains, and how a community of sophisticated artists flourished there during the period, are explored in this compelling new analysis.

The artist milking "Daisy" at his Tryon vineyard, 1925.

Handsomely produced and with copious illustrations, *Paris and Tryon* describes the remarkable vitality of the cosmopolitan Tryon colony, and challenges common assumptions about fine art in the South before World War II.

Michael McCue has previously authored *Homer Ellertson (1892-1935)*; *Lawrence Mazzanovich: Impressionist Paintings of Tryon* [Asheville Art Museum]; and *Tryon Artists 1892-1942*.

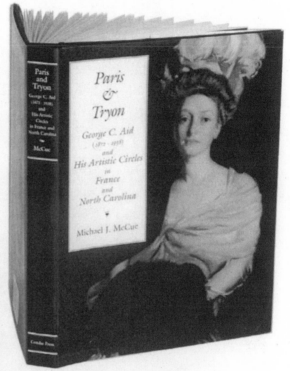

Paris and Tryon:
George C. Aid (1872 - 1938)
and His Artistic Circles
in France and North Carolina

quarto, 221 pp.
275 b&w + 41 color illustrations
ISBN 0-9726801-1-x. $65 + $6 s&h

· CONDAR · PRESS ·

PO Box 250 · Columbus · North Carolina 28722
828-894-8383 ext 239 · www.condar.com/press